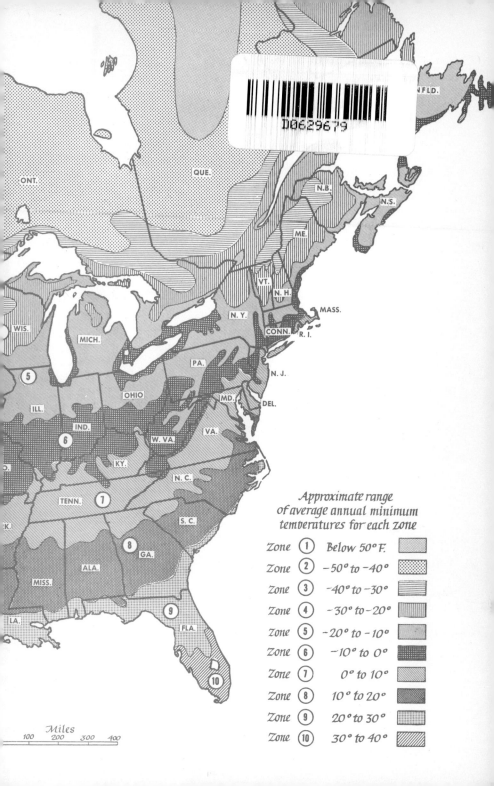

Approximate range
of average annual minimum
temperatures for each zone

Zone ① Below 50° F.
Zone ② −50° to −40°
Zone ③ −40° to −30°
Zone ④ −30° to −20°
Zone ⑤ −20° to −10°
Zone ⑥ −10° to 0°
Zone ⑦ 0° to 10°
Zone ⑧ 10° to 20°
Zone ⑨ 20° to 30°
Zone ⑩ 30° to 40°

Miles
100   200   300   400

D0629679

# THE CONCISE ENCYCLOPEDIA
# OF FAVORITE FLOWERING SHRUBS

# THE
# Concise Encyclopedia
# of Favorite Flowering
# SHRUBS

## A HUNDRED FLOWERING SHRUBS
## SELECTED FOR CONTEMPORARY
## HOME GARDEN PLANTING

*Illustrated by Katharine Burton*

## MARJORIE J. DIETZ

EDITOR, FLOWER GROWER, THE HOME
GARDEN MAGAZINE; AUTHOR, THE CONCISE
ENCYCLOPEDIA OF FAVORITE FLOWERS

Doubleday & Company, Inc.
Garden City, New York

Library of Congress Catalog Card Number 63–11669
Copyright © 1963 by Marjorie J. Dietz
All Rights Reserved
Printed in the United States of America

# CONTENTS

# FOREWORD

MONTAGUE FREE

In and out of bloom, flowering shrubs give the garden the permanency that must prevail as a background for the ever-changing scene engendered by the shorter-lived plants.

This encyclopedia of flowering shrubs, a companion volume to *The Concise Encyclopedia of Favorite Flowers,* helps today's home gardener make a wise selection. For each shrub the author gives an over-all picture of the plant, a description of its flowers, its native habitat and its cultural requirements. The uses and growth habits are explained and its major periods of seasonal interest detailed. Hardiness zones are given for each shrub— you will find your area indicated on the Plant Hardiness Zone Map on the end papers of the book.

The author writes from first-hand experience gained through observations in her own garden on Long Island, as well as through her travels both in this country and abroad. I first had the pleasure of working with Marjorie on the *Home Garden Magazine* and now at *Flower Grower Magazine,* the *Home Garden Magazine* having merged with *Flower Grower* some years ago. In her capacity as Editor she is especially qualified to understand the interests and problems of the home gardener and the format of her book is such that any home gardener can readily find the information he is seeking.

Take Spice-Bush or Benzoin for example: first we learn how to pronounce Lindera, the Latin name. Then in the opening paragraph we get an over-all picture of this shrub and learn that its flowers are not spectacular, that it is a native in wet soil so one can plant it without having to worry about good drainage. The uses and growth habits are explained. Flowers open before the leaves, which is fortunate because if they had to compete with the foliage they would not be noticeable. The scarlet berries are interesting but you should be certain to have a plant that carries both male and female blossoms. It is hardy to Zone 4. With the index you can look up a shrub by either its common or botanical name.

# THE CONCISE ENCYCLOPEDIA
# OF FAVORITE FLOWERING SHRUBS

# ANDROMEDA

TYPE Broadleaf evergreen
FAMILY *Ericaceae* (Ehr-ik-*ay*-see-ee)
GENUS *Pieris* (*Pye*-er-iss)
SPECIES *floribunda* (floh-rib-*bund*-uh), *Forresti* (*For*-res-tye),
*japonica* (jap-*pon*-ik-uh), *taiwanensis* (tye-won-*en*-siss)
ZONE 5, 6

Andromeda is a near-perfect flowering shrub. A member of the Heath family, which includes Azaleas and Rhododendrons, it is a good companion plant for these as well as for other shrubs of the same family.

USES   In foundation plantings around both contemporary and traditional houses; in mixed shrub borders and groupings; as accent specimens in a variety of garden situations; as companion plants to other evergreen shrubs in open, informal woodland or naturalistic settings. Both foliage and flowers are attractive in flower arrangements, and flowers can be forced readily.

HABIT OF GROWTH   Compact, bushy shrubs, sometimes quite oval in outline, sometimes gracefully irregular; height between 3 and 10 feet, depending on species and location.

FLOWERS   White, urn-shaped flowers, about ¼ inch long, in panicles from 3 to 6 inches long, at the ends of branches; appearing in April, they often last well into May. From a short distance, Andromeda's flower panicles resemble the sprays of Lily-of-the-valley. Flower buds are remarkably showy in winter.

FOLIAGE   Evergreen, alternate leaves, about 3 inches long, glossy, and always effective. New leaf growth of some species in the spring is dark red or bronze, contrasting pleasantly with the bright green of older leaves.

ASSETS   An outstanding landscaping shrub where hardy, and attractive at all seasons. The Japanese Andromeda (*Pieris japonica*) can be the perfect solution when one choice shrub is sought for a prominent position.

FAULTS   Andromeda must have acid soil. Flower buds of Japanese Andromeda will winterkill when temperatures remain at extremely low levels. Japanese Andromeda can be made unsightly by attacks of the lace bug, especially when grown in too sunny a location.

CULTURE   All species of Andromeda thrive under the same soil conditions as Azaleas and Rhododendrons. Soil must be acid, well drained, and full of humus. Add quantities of peat moss, leafmold, or compost to the planting hole so that the mixture contains about one-half humus. Part shade is best. Plants growing in full sun are more susceptible to lace-bug infestation. Don't crowd Andromeda—each plant should stand alone and be permitted to assume its individual shape without being crowded by other shrubs. Andromeda is easy to grow from seed sown indoors in November in sphagnum moss which, after being soaked, is covered by a tent of polyethylene. Seedlings can be set out in coldframe or protected ground in spring.

PESTS AND DISEASES   The *lace bug* is a sucking insect which turns the leaves of the Japanese Andromeda yellow or mottled gray. Keep plants out of full sun and hot, dry, and airless situations. Spray with lindane or malathion at two-week intervals, starting in early May, for several weeks if this pest is present.

SPECIES AND VARIETIES   *Pieris floribunda.* Mountain Andromeda. Native to the Allegheny Mountains from Virginia to Georgia and hardy to Zone 5. Compact, slow growing, perhaps less formal than other species. Its flower panicles are upright rather than drooping.
*P. Forresti.* Native to western China and a recent introduction. New growth is salmon-red. Height from 5 to 8 feet. Erect flower clusters 4 to 6 inches high. Hardiness undetermined, but it is now being grown in the Pacific Northwest and is probably too tender for most northeastern gardens.
*P. japonica.* Japanese Andromeda. An aristocratic shrub in every detail. Native to Japan. Its long-lasting flower panicles are 6 inches long, often start to flower in early April. Average height is 5 feet but it can reach 10 feet or more in very favorable locations. Hardy to Zone 6, where it endures winter temperatures to 10 degrees below zero. Some nurseries offer variegated forms.
*P. taiwanensis.* Formosa Andromeda. Similar to Japanese Andromeda. Its nodding flowers are slightly larger and are carried on shorter panicles, erect rather than drooping.

# *AZALEA*

TYPE Evergreen and deciduous
FAMILY *Ericaceae* (Ehr-ik-*ay*-see-ee)
GENUS *Rhododendron* (Roh-doh-*den*-dron)
SPECIES *arborescens* (ar-bor-*ress*-senz), *calendulaceum* (kal-en-dew-*lay*-see-um), *indicum* (*inn*-dik-um), *japonicum* (jap-*pon*-ik-um), *Kaempferi* (*Kemp*-fur-eye), *molle* (*moll*-ee), *mucronatum* (mew-kron-*nay*-tum), *nudiflorum* (new-dif-*floh*-rum), *obtusum* (ob-*tew*-sum), *occidentale* (ok-sid-en-*tay*-lee), *roseum* (*roh*-zee-um), *Schlippenbachi* (Shlip-en-*bahk*-eye), *vaseyi* (*vay*-see-eye), *viscosum* (viss-*koh*-sum)
ZONE See descriptions of species, below

To many, the Azalea is the supreme flowering shrub, its closest rival being the Rhododendron; but this, of course, is not a real competition, as the Azalea is in the genus *Rhododendron*. (While the Azalea and the Rhododendron are true "blood relatives" because they are in the same genus, it is simpler to deal with them separately.) There are Azalea species native to North America, to Asia, and to Eastern Europe. From these has come a wealth of varieties and hybrids, not always but sometimes more outstanding than the parents.

USES  For foundation plantings; along walks and drives; in rock gardens; as ground covers for taller Azaleas and related plants; on slopes and banks; around terraces, pools and ponds; in shrub borders; in woodland beneath tall trees such as Oaks, or as underplantings to or around smaller trees such as Dogwood and evergreens. There are less hardy Azaleas that can be grown as house plants or in the home greenhouse in the North. The Japanese have found that Azaleas are wonderful for the art of Bonsai.

HABIT OF GROWTH  Variation is the rule. Azaleas can be tall and upright as well as tall and spreading; they can be of medium height, or dwarf and lower-growing than many familiar ground-cover plants. The Azalea illustrated here is typical of the deciduous Azalea, such as an EXBURY or MOLLIS hybrid.

FLOWERS  Usually trumpet- or funnel-shaped, with prominent stamens, or bowl-shaped, as in many evergreen types. They may be single, or double, or hose-in-hose, that is, with one "flower" inside another. Some are decidedly fragrant. Some have flowers that appear before the new foliage breaks out, while in other deciduous types the flowers appear after the new leaves or simultaneously with them. Colors include just about every one except true blue, and petals may be solid, streaked, blotched, or in combinations. Size of individual flowers varies greatly from type to type, as do the numbers produced on a typical plant. Some of the evergreen Azaleas are literally smothered with flowers, while in others flowers may appear in more modest numbers.

FOLIAGE   There are Azaleas which are deciduous—that is, which lose their leaves in winter—as well as those that are evergreen or semi-evergreen. The alternate leaves range in length from 1 inch or less to 6 inches or so, depending on the type. Fall coloring of some of the deciduous sorts may be outstanding.

ASSETS   Azaleas are magnificent in flower. By choosing early-blooming as well as midseason and late types, one may have a season of bloom extending from early spring to midsummer. The evergreen Azaleas offer year-long landscaping value. While not all Azaleas are suited to all climates and all soil conditions, there are kinds for the deep South as well as the North. In general, they are easy to grow and require little maintenance. The tremendous range in their size, habit of growth, and flower color offers great challenge to the hybridizer, nurseryman, designer, and home landscaper as well as the hobby gardener.

FAULTS   The only possible fault with Azaleas is that they require acid soil. Some of the evergreen kinds, particularly the HINODEGIRI Azalea, have been overused while better kinds have been neglected.

CULTURE   Azaleas will not tolerate hot, dry soils that are alkaline. They do thrive in peaty soils that have a pH value between 4.5 and 5.5 and are full of organic matter—leafmold, decaying wood, old roots. Those who live in areas where Oaks, Blueberries, and other acid-soil inhabitants grow naturally will have no trouble on the score of soil acidity. Others, provided their soil is not outright alkaline, can have soil tests made (state experiment stations, county agents, and private soil laboratories offer this service) in order to determine its suitability. Or the gardener can do it himself with a soil-testing kit, and amend the soil according to results. The best additive is peat moss, easily bought in bales or bags. The next ideal humus source is leaf-mold. If soil tests show a pH reading over 5, add at least 50 per cent of peat moss or leafmold to the soil, which should also have an acid rating. Flowers of sulphur or ferrous sulphate (Copperas) are the chemicals usually recommended to acidify soil when tests indicate their need. Heavy clay soils with poor underdrainage—even though acid—are not suitable. Where such soils exist one solution is to plant Azaleas in raised beds in which the clay soil has been lightened by the addition of peat moss. Sandy soils are satisfactory for Azaleas if they have been bolstered by the addition of the necessary moisture-retentive humus materials—peat moss, for example. Most Azaleas thrive in full sun, although light shade is satisfactory. The deciduous Azaleas, especially, need plenty of sun for flowering, while the evergreen types, especially the late-flowering ones, prefer high shade like that given by Oaks and Pines. Azaleas, in company with Rhododendrons, are perfectly suited to a thin woodland setting; the somewhat sparser flowering of some of the evergreen types which may receive more shade than is considered ideal can be even more charming than the blankets of color made in sunnier locations. Fortunately, Azaleas are shallow-rooted and can be moved without difficulty if they are in unsuitable spots. While protection from strong, sweeping winds is essential, good air drainage is desirable. Fertilize Azaleas in early spring with cottonseed meal, an organic acid fertilizer, or use commercial fertilizers especially formulated for acid-soil plants. Well-rotted manure that has virtually become humus can be safely used as a mulch or mixed with soil at the time of planting. Azaleas should be planted or transplanted in the spring or fall, and it is perfectly safe to do this even when they are in full flower. It is important not to plant too deeply—the crown, the place where roots and stems meet, should be level with the soil surface.

PRUNING  Azaleas need little pruning other than the removal of dead wood and the occasional cutting back of growth that is out of bounds. Some of the deciduous types can be encouraged to send up new shoots around the base of the plant each year if old, leggy, less productive stems are cut off.

PROPAGATION  Part of the fun in growing Azaleas for the amateur is the ease with which they can be increased. Most of the evergreen types root quickly from cuttings taken in early summer. Use the new growth, making the cuttings a few inches long; insert in a mixture of peat moss and gritty sand in a flat box or container that can be covered with polyethylene. The cuttings and rooting medium should be well soaked before the plastic is put in place. The container should be left outdoors in shade and will need no additional watering until the rooted cuttings are removed in three to five weeks' time. The cuttings are then planted in rows in the open ground or, preferably, in a coldframe, in peaty soil kept watered and lightly shaded. Many Azaleas naturally form layers, and these rooted plant parts can be cut from the parent, preferably in spring to midsummer, and replanted. Other Azaleas can be made to form layers by pegging a pliant branch to the soil with a stone or a hairpin. A third method of propagation is by seeds. They should be sown in late fall or early winter in shredded sphagnum moss, which has been thoroughly moistened, in flats or smaller containers and covered with a tent of polyethylene. In a north window, at a temperature of 60 degrees at night and from 65 to 70 during the day, the seeds germinate quickly. After the first "true" leaves appear, the seedlings can be transplanted into flats containing a mixture of 2 parts topsoil or leafmold, 2 parts Michigan peat, and 1 part sand. Or use the "prepared," sterilized potting mixtures sold for such house plants as Gardenias and African-violets. The young Azalea seedlings can be gradually exposed to partial morning sun, then placed outdoors, in their flats, after frost danger has passed. They can stay in their flats until the following spring or can be lined out in a nursery area; in either case they need protection from full sunlight.


PESTS AND DISEASES   *Chlorosis,* identified by bright yellow foliage with the veins outlined in green, is most often related to a plant's inability to utilize iron. Iron chelates (Sequestrene), used according to directions on the package, usually correct the trouble. *Flower spot* or *petal blight,* common in the South and now creeping northward, is a fungus disease that attacks evergreen Azaleas; it can be serious, spoiling the flowers in a few days by turning them mushy. Control is to spray the swelling buds and opening flowers three times a week with Dithane D-14, following directions on the container.

SPECIES AND VARIETIES *Rhododendron arborescens.* Smooth or Sweet Azalea. White, fragrant flowers, after the leaves, late (June) on 8-foot plants. Native to upland woods and mountains from Pennsylvania to Georgia and Tennessee. Useful for naturalizing in light woods or as background in shrub borders. Zone 5.

*R. calendulaceum.* Flame Azalea. Orange to yellow and scarlet flowers, 2 inches across, on 4- to 10-foot plants, after the leaves appear, in mid-spring (May–June). Native to New York, Pennsylvania, and south to Georgia. Great variations in flower color, form, and size. Choice. Zone 5.

*R. indicum.* Macrantha Azalea. Rose or scarlet flowers, 2½ inches across, on spreading, twiggy plants, up to 6 feet. Native to Japan. Foliage evergreen. Blooms in late June. Hardy to New York City.

*R. japonicum.* Japanese Azalea. Orange, yellow, red flowers, 2–3 inches across, before the leaves open, on 6-foot plants in mid-May. Native to Japan. Very hardy (proven at Rochester, N.Y.; Boston; Ithaca, N.Y.). Quick and easy from seed for the home gardener. Zone 5.

*R. Kaempferi.* Torch Azalea. Flowers salmon-red, 2 inches across, on 3- to 5-foot plants, in late May. Foliage deciduous or semi-evergreen. Grow in part shade or flowers will fade. Native to Japan. Zone 5.

*R. molle.* Chinese Azalea. Similar to but less hardy than Japanese Azalea. Zone 6.

*R. mucronatum.* Snow Azalea. Greenish-white flowers, 2 inches across, fragrant, on spreading plants up to 4 feet high. Foliage semi-evergreen. Native to Japan. Hardy to New York City if grown in protected areas. Very choice. Zone 6.

*R. nudiflorum.* Pinxterbloom. Pink or white flowers, very fragrant, in late May, on 3- to 6-foot plants. Native to dry, open woods of northeastern U.S. Suitable for naturalizing. Zone 4.

*R. obtusum.* Kurume Azalea. Flower color ranges from salmon to magenta and scarlet. Very spreading, floriferous plants with evergreen or deciduous foliage, up to 3 feet tall. Many varieties and hybrids; not generally considered reliably hardy beyond New York City. Native to Japan. Zone 6.

*R. occidentale.* Western Azalea. White or pink flowers, in mid-May, as leaves open, on 8-foot plants. Native to mountains of West Coast and not reliably hardy in the Northeast.

*R. roseum.* Roseshell or Piedmont Azalea. Bright pink flowers, 1½ inches across, very fragrant, in late May as leaves open, on 2- to 8-foot plants. Native to Northeast. Very hardy. Zone 4. Useful in shrub border or in open woodlands, and stands sun and wind.

*R. Schlippenbachi.* Royal Azalea. Pale-rose to pink flowers, 3 inches across, mildly fragrant, in late May, on tall plants (to 10 feet). Very hardy. Outstanding foliage color in fall. Zone 5.

*R. vaseyi.* Pinkshell Azalea. Rose flowers, 2 inches across, in early May, on 5- to 15-foot plants. Native to Blue Ridge Mountains. Very hardy. Colorful fall foliage. Zone 5.

*R. viscosum.* Swamp Azalea. Swamp-honeysuckle. White flowers, fragrant, sticky to touch, on 4- to 8-foot plants, in July and August. Native to swamplands in eastern U.S. from Maine to South Carolina and west to Ohio. Zone 4.

HYBRIDS AND VARIETIES  The following groups can only be listed here without description because of the great number of plants included: EXBURY HYBRIDS, GHENT HYBRIDS, GLENDALE HYBRIDS, KNAP HILL HYBRIDS, KAEMPFERI HYBRIDS, MOLLIS, VUYK HYBRIDS. For details of these as well as many others, consult nursery catalogues and books devoted specifically to Azaleas.

# BARBERRY

TYPE Deciduous and evergreen
FAMILY *Berberidaceae* (Ber-ber-id-*day*-see-ee)
GENUS *Berberis* (*Ber*-ber-iss)
SPECIES *Darwini* (*Dar*-win-eye), *Gagnepaini* (Gag-nep-*pyen*-eye),
*Julianae* (Jew-lee-*ay*-nee), *koreana* (koh-ree-*ay*-nuh), *Thunbergi*
(*Thun*-berj-eye), *triacanthophora* (trye-ak-anth-*off*-or-ruh), *ver-
ruculosa* (vehr-rook-yew-*loh*-suh)
ZONE See descriptions of species, below

Although the various kinds of Barberry shrubs are invaluable for landscape use, they are not especially noted for their flowers, nor do all of them possess exceptionally showy fruit. The few included here are the most outstanding for floral beauty. The Barberries are native to Asia, South America, and Europe, although one species, European or Common Barberry (*Berberis vulgaris*), has become so widely established in the wild in North America that it appears to be native.

USES   Traditionally as hedges, really as barriers because of the sharp spines on their branches. Some of the evergreen Barberries, such as *B. Julianae,* deserve less hackneyed placement. Use as a specimen, either in groups of three or four or singly; as background or middle-section subjects for shrub borders, as companion plants to such broad-leaved evergreens as Rhododendrons. The Wintergreen Barberry (*B. Julianae*) makes an effective screen and is at the same time a handsome background for other shrubs or flowering plants.

HABIT OF GROWTH   Dense, upright plants that will make spreading or arching growth if given the space. Their stems and twigs, often bright yellow, are covered with brown or reddish thorns or spines, varying in arrangement and length according to the species.

FLOWERS   The yellow or orange flowers appear in spring and, though small, are usually borne in sufficient numbers to make a good show. They are usually yellow, appear singly or in clusters, and possess a waxy, delicate beauty. The berries that follow vary in shape and color, some being oblong or oval, and red, yellow, or black.

FOLIAGE   The leaves are alternate, deciduous, or evergreen, and contribute greatly to the attractiveness of these shrubs. In the evergreen Barberries, the leaves are Hollylike in appearance. Fall coloring of some of the deciduous Barberries (especially *B. Thunbergi*) can be spectacular. There are also varieties with purple foliage.

ASSETS  The Barberries are easy to grow, and there are species that are hardy for most northern areas. They make formidable barriers that can be attractive as well. The fruit, often very showy, can be long lasting on some species, while the spiny foliage of some of the evergreen Barberries makes them almost as desirable as Hollies and Rhododendrons.

FAULTS  Other shrubs give better floral displays than most of the Barberries, which flower at a time when there is no dearth of good material. One species, the Japanese Barberry (*B. Thunbergi*), has been overplanted, often in situations where it never gets a chance to show its graceful habit. (Many Barberry species are alternate hosts to the black stem rust of wheat, but the species recommended here are apparently not susceptible to this disease.)

CULTURE  Barberries prefer full sun but can tolerate light shade. An average soil, even somewhat dry, will give good results, although the evergreen kinds have more need of an even moisture supply than the deciduous species. All Barberries respond to good care—soil well supplied with organic matter, water during periods of drought, and space in which to grow. This is especially true of the familiar Japanese Barberry, which can assume its rounded, spreading form when it is planted in situations suitable for any shrub, not in soil that is inert and like concrete or in a site lacking light or air. Barberries are generally free from pests and diseases.

PRUNING  The evergreen Barberries require little pruning other than occasional removal of wayward shoots and branches. The deciduous Barberries can be pruned if their special use, such as in a hedge, requires it. Whole branches can be removed, or merely sections. Plants can also be sheared in the same manner as Box, although such formal shaping is neither especially desirable nor now in vogue. Barberries, at least those discussed here, are most attractive when they are permitted to assume their natural spreading shape.

SPECIES AND VARIETIES *Berberis Darwini.* Darwin's Barberry. Evergreen, native to Chile and popular in the British Isles. In this country it is hardy to Zone 8 (10–20 degrees) and therefore of value in California and the South. Evergreen, Hollylike foliage and showy yellow-orange flowers make it one of the choicest Barberries.

*B. Gagnepaini.* Black Barberry. Narrow, evergreen leaves and bright yellow flowers to ½ inch long, in clusters, followed by black berries. This species will reach 6 feet. Hardy to Zone 6.

*B. Julianae.* Wintergreen Barberry. One of the best, it is hardy, evergreen, and bears clusters of showy yellow flowers in early May that are followed by black berries. Widely available; still not planted enough. Use for accent, specimen, foundation, or in mixed planting as in shrub border. Hardy to Zone 5.

*B. koreana.* Korean Barberry. Deciduous species similar to the outlawed Common Barberry. It has yellow flowers in hanging clusters that are quite showy, and bright red, long-lasting berries. Makes a good hedge plant. Zone 6.

*B. Thunbergi.* Japanese Barberry. This deciduous Barberry, with rather insignificant yellow and red flowers, has showy red berries, can be striking when well grown. Its fall foliage color is beautiful. Many varieties available, some with red or purple foliage. For a hedge, plant 2 feet apart. Height 7 feet. Very hardy. Zone 3.

*B. triacanthophora.* Threespine Barberry. Evergreen Barberry from China, with attractive, spreading habit to 4 feet, making it suitable for foundation planting. Its flowers are white and red, ¼ inch wide, in clusters. Fruit is blue-black. Hardy to Zone 6.

*B. verruculosa.* Warty Barberry. An outstanding evergreen Barberry from China, with spiny Hollylike leaves of leathery texture which are almost white underneath. It has showy orange-yellow flowers, about ½ inch wide, making this one of the best Barberries for floral effect. Growth is spreading, with eventual height only 3 or 4 feet. Hardy to Zone 3 with protection.

## *BEACH PLUM*

TYPE Deciduous
FAMILY *Rosaceae* (Roz-*ay*-see-ee)
GENUS *Prunus* (*Proon*-us)
SPECIES *maritima* (mar-*rit*-im-uh)
ZONE 4

In full bloom in spring, this native shrub turns East Coast sand dunes and roadsides into a wintery, snowy landscape, so abundant and pure white are its flowers. It is found from New Brunswick to Virginia along the Atlantic Coast.

USES   For seashore gardens and windswept locations, on banks, as an informal hedge or barrier, or as an attractive accent plant. Elsewhere, it can be used in naturalistic plantings. Its fruit makes a delicious jelly or jam.

HABIT OF GROWTH   It naturally makes a suckering straggling shrub, sometimes treelike, up to 6 feet. When planted in good soil it may reach 10 feet.

FLOWERS   Snow-white flowers ½ inch across crowd the stems from top to bottom. The blue-purple fruit (sometimes dark red), about ¾ inch to an inch across, makes almost as showy an effect as the flowers; ripens in late summer.

FOLIAGE   Leaves 2 inches long, deep green.

ASSETS   Its ability to thrive in poor soil, even mostly sand, in exposed locations makes this an important shrub for seaside gardeners who have too few shrubs among which to choose. Also its showy flowers, lovely enough to attract gardeners in more favorable locations.

FAULTS   Difficult to transplant when growing wild. This shrub will grow out of bounds in a small garden when placed in rich soil.

CULTURE   The Beach Plum has few requirements except good drainage and full sun. When removed from its rugged dune site, it grows quickly and may become a small tree. By light pruning in early spring it can be trained to a regular shape or a more picturesque outline, whichever is preferred. To encourage abundant flowering, cut back old branches occasionally and remove dead wood. A few New England nurseries carry improved varieties.

# BEAUTY-BUSH

TYPE Deciduous
FAMILY *Caprifoliaceae* (Kap-rif-fol-lee-*ay*-see-ee)
GENUS *Kolkwitzia* (Kol-*kwits*-ee-uh)
SPECIES *amabilis* (am-*mab*-il-iss)
ZONE 5

The flowers of Beauty-bush are subtle when compared with other shrubs that bloom in June, yet they are in such numbers as to make a handsome display. It was introduced by E. H. Wilson from central China and has been available since the 1920s.

**FLOWERS**   Soft pink bells with a yellow throat, about ½ inch long, and borne in pairs. They are followed by bristly seeds.

**FOLIAGE**   Pleasant gray-green leaves with a hairy texture. They are opposite, about 3 inches long.

**HABIT OF GROWTH**   Upright shrub with arching branches, to about 8 feet, although mature specimens may reach 15 feet. It will spread to a space equal to its height.

**ASSETS**   Beauty-bush's profuse flowers, its foliage, which remains attractive all summer—even under drought conditions— its exfoliating bark, which is of some interest during the winter, and its undemanding culture, all combine to make this shrub the nearly perfect plant. It is listed by all nurseries.

**FAULTS**   None, really, except that it does need room, a factor that might exclude its use for small suburban properties.

**USES**   Best as a background shrub for a mixed shrub planting or, where space permits, as a boundary shrub. It flowers at the same time as the late Lilac, *Syringa villosa,* many Mock-oranges, Spireas, and Weigela, and blends well with all of these. Sprays of the flowering branches are desirable in flower arrangements.

**CULTURE**   Beauty-bush has no special demands and even grows well in dry, sandy soil. It is tolerant of heat and wind.

**PRUNING**   Occasional thinning of branches, at ground level, after flowering.

# BLUEBERRY

TYPE Deciduous
FAMILY *Ericaceae* (Ehr-ik-*ay*-see-ee)
GENUS *Vaccinium* (Vak-*sin*-ee-um)
SPECIES *corymbosum* (kor-im-*boh*-sum)
ZONE 4

Although best known for its attractive and delicious berries, the Highbush Blueberry has appeal as a flowering shrub when its branches are strung with urn-shaped flowers in spring. It is native from Maine to Florida and Louisiana.

USES  For their fruit (usually in rows or as a border to vegetable garden). Also as informal hedges; in mixed shrub borders, where they make natural companions to Azaleas and Rhododendrons; as underplantings to Oaks or Birches; or simply as rugged dwellers in any open woodland. They are generally too large for foundation plantings, but can be transitional fillers between foundation plantings and related nearby groupings.

HABIT OF GROWTH  A sturdy frame of intricate branches which can make a distinctively rounded form or an irregular bush, depending on exposure and training. Eventual height can be 10 to 12 feet; plants will be much lower in full sun. The winter silhouette, with dark-red coloring of new twig growth, is effective.

FLOWERS  Clusters of white or pink-tinged bells, about ⅓ inch long, in early May, usually before the leaves have opened fully.

FOLIAGE  Alternate leaves, about 3 inches long, which turn to glorious shades of orange, red, and scarlet in the fall. As with Enkianthus, whose flowers are a larger version of the Blueberry's, the autumn foliage coloring is a dividend.

ASSETS  Hardiness, tolerance of boggy soil conditions as well as drier sites (so long as soil is acid), interesting spring flowers followed by edible fruits, outstanding fall foliage color, and an often picturesque winter outline.

FAULTS  The Highbush Blueberry probably offers little to the owner of a small property. And, of course, it will not thrive unless the soil is acid.

CULTURE  Blueberries, in common with other plants in the same family, must have acid soil. While Highbush Blueberries in the wild often grow in very moist or even boggy woodland, they adapt readily to drier soil as long as it is acid and contains plenty of organic matter. Peat moss, readily available, is the best material to use. Plants will grow in sun or light shade.

PRUNING  Blueberries grown for ornament require little pruning compared to those grown for fruit. In the former case pruning is only necessary for shaping and training and can be done in early spring. For fruit production techniques consult books on fruit growing and bulletins from state agricultural stations.

VARIETIES  There are many named varieties of Highbush Blueberries which have been developed and selected for superior fruit production; any of these can be used for landscaping purposes. Plants of *Vaccinium corymbosum* can be collected from the wild, too, and will make very satisfactory ornamentals.

# BLUE-SPIREA

TYPE Deciduous
FAMILY *Verbenaceae* (Ver-ben-*nay*-see-ee)
GENUS *Caryopteris* (Kay-ree-*op*-ter-iss)
SPECIES *incana* (in-*kay*-nuh)
ZONE 5

Neither a Spirea nor related to it, this shrub does somewhat resemble some kinds of Spirea. Perhaps its other common name, Bluebeard, is more appropriate, as it is a fair description of the flower clusters. Caryopteris, by whatever name, is native to China.

USES  Think of the Blue-spirea as a rather bushy perennial that flowers about the same time as Phlox and you have the key to its value. Several plants can be grouped in front of taller, more substantial shrubs to give mid- and late-summer color. The flowers of the Blue-spirea offer good contrast in both their color and form to any Roses, such as floribunda types, or some ever-blooming shrub Roses, as well as shrubs like Hypericum, Potentilla, Rose of Sharon, Vitex. It also is not out of place in a flower garden where it combines and contrasts well with both annuals and perennials. The flowers are wonderful for arrangements.

HABIT OF GROWTH  It makes a mound of slender stems, usually from 1½ to 2 feet high. The stems may die back to ground level, as do those of most perennials, but new ones shoot up from the crown in the spring.

FLOWERS  Clusters of fuzzy, lavender-blue flowers on short stalks from the leaf axils up the entire stem, starting in mid-summer and lasting into the fall.

FOLIAGE  Opposite, toothed leaves, 3 inches long, slightly aromatic and silvery green.

ASSETS  Hardiness and late summer flowering are its assets.

FAULTS  Without its flowers, this shrub is not of great landscape value if one has space for only a few shrubs.

CULTURE  Easy-to-grow in average or even sandy soils, the Blue-spirea does need full sun. If stems are winterkilled, cut them back at the base where new stem growth will appear. Even when no die-back of stems occurs, it is recommended that they be shortened somewhat in the spring to make stocky growth.

NAMED VARIETIES   Caryopteris BLUE MIST: Apparently of hybrid origin, the full name of this is often listed as *C. clandonensis* (*incana* X *mongholica*) BLUE MIST. Powdery blue flowers on stems from 2 to 4 feet, beginning in midsummer. HEAVENLY BLUE: (Plant Patent No. 1091) An introduction from Wayside Gardens. It reaches a height of 24 inches, forming a mound of about the same width, and produces its deep lavender-blue flowers in late summer.

# *BOTTLEBRUSH BUCKEYE*

TYPE Deciduous
FAMILY *Hippocastanaceae* (Hip-poh-kass-tan-*nay*-see-ee)
GENUS *Aesculus* (*Ess*-kew-lus)
SPECIES *parviflora* (par-vif-*floh*-ruh)
ZONE 5

Most Buckeyes, or Horse-chestnuts, are majestic flowering trees, but some species are true shrubs; one of these is the Bottlebrush Buckeye, native from South Carolina to Alabama and Florida. It is perfectly hardy and can take temperatures to 20 degrees below zero.

USES   It needs lots of room. Use as large accents in naturalistic plantings where it can spread at will, or in extensive lawn areas.

HABIT OF GROWTH   Upright, many-stemmed shrub to 8 feet; may soon form a spreading clump because of the tendency of the branches to layer. Clumps eventually may spread to a diameter twice their height.

FLOWERS   Attractive, upright panicles, 1 foot long, of tiny white flowers with prominent stamens; blooms in July and August.

FOLIAGE   Five to seven leaflets, typical of the Horse-chestnut; although rather large and coarse, foliage makes an attractive background for the flower spikes. Leaves turn yellow in the fall.

ASSETS   The handsome flowers in summer and the undemanding nature of this shrub make it valuable for gardeners with extensive properties.

FAULTS   Too large and spreading for small places.

CULTURE   Although this Buckeye will grow in average soils, the best growth will take place in rich, moist situations in full sun. It needs no special pruning and is easily increased by removal of suckering branches in spring or fall.

# *BROOM*

TYPE Evergreen and deciduous
FAMILY *Leguminosae* (Leg-yew-min-*noh*-see)
GENUS *Cytisus* (*Sit*-iss-us)
SPECIES *Battendieri* (Bah-ten-dee-*ehr*-eye), *Burkwoodi* (*Burk*-wood-eye), *Kewensis* (Kew-*en*-siss), *nigricans* (*nye*-grik-anz), *praecox* (*pree*-cox), *purgans* (*purr*-ganz), *purpureus* (pur-*pew*-ree-us), *scoparius* (scop-*pay*-ree-us)
ZONE See descriptions of species, below

Brooms can be everything to the gardener who can give them the right climate and situation. None are native to North America, but the bonny Scotch Broom *C. scoparius* has become naturalized in many areas of the East, West, and the upper South.

USES   Brooms vary in height and habit but many are suited to sunny, dry pockets of a rock garden as well as to larger areas such as slopes and banks; some will cascade over walls. The Genista (which see) of florists is *Cytisus canariensis,* a popular pot plant. The taller, spreading types of Broom can be planted in a sunny border among other shrubs, either grouped in the foreground or rear, according to the type selected; or, grow them for their own sake as accent, screen or informal hedging.

HABIT OF GROWTH   Brooms may be low and even ground hugging, or may grow to heights of from 6 to 9 feet; their branches may be upright or pendulous, willowy or stiff. In the favored climates of the Pacific Northwest and the British Isles, the tall Brooms become treelike, with thick trunks.

FLOWERS   Showy, Pealike flowers in racemes, usually very fragrant, and borne in spring or early summer. Colors, bright yellow, cream and lemon yellow, as well as maroon-red or purple.

FOLIAGE   The leaves—evergreen, semi-evergreen, or deciduous—can be so small as to be scalelike or can be large, consisting of three silvery-gray leaflets, as in *Cytisus Battendieri.*

ASSETS   Bright-colored flowers, usually fragrant, making a mass of color, whether on the low-growing plants or the tall types. Also, the green stems and twigs, which can light up the winter landscape as effectively as the red- and yellow-twigged dogwoods. A third consideration is the Broom's tolerance for sunny, sandy, dry situations.

FAULTS   On the fringes of their climatic tolerances, Brooms may winterkill to the extent that they appear straggly; or, at the other extreme, they may thrive so robustly as to outgrow their site. Brooms, like so many legumes, can hardly be transplanted, so once a plant has outgrown its space, hacking it out may be the only solution.

CULTURE    Full sun and well-drained soil. They tolerate dry, sandy soils of low fertility that would be rejected by most plants. Even so, it is a good idea to add peat moss in the planting hole to get them off to a good start. Brooms are difficult to move, so most nurseries supply small, pot-grown plants. Most Brooms will eventually cover an area two or three times their height.

PRUNING    Immediately after flowering. With most Brooms, it is a shearing process rather than one of removing individual stems. All Brooms can be kept dense and shapely by an annual cutting back—but to last year's wood only; in fact, this annual pruning seems to be essential to keep them tidy.

SPECIES AND VARIETIES    *Cytisus Battendieri.* Native to Algiers and well known in England, it has only recently become available in the United States. Hardy in sunny, protected sites in Zone 6 (−10 to 0 degrees). Very fragrant, tight racemes of golden-yellow flowers in early summer. Silvery trifoliate leaves on stems to 6 feet or more. Tends to sucker. Very hard to transplant.

*C. Burkwoodi.* English hybrid, to 3–4 feet, with maroon and red flowers. It has tiny leaves and evergreen stems. Hardy in Zones 6 and 7.

*C. Kewensis.* Kew Broom. Pale yellow flowers in mid-spring on evergreen stems only 6 inches high; may spread to form a mat 6 feet across. Excellent as ground cover and for large rock gardens. Hardy Zone 7 (0 to 10 degrees).

*C. nigricans.* Spike Broom. Showy yellow, fragrant flowers in summer on 3–5 foot stems. Trifoliate gray leaves. One of the hardiest Brooms, it will thrive where winter temperatures regularly fall below zero. Zones 5, 6.

*C. praecox.* Warminster Broom. Choice and more readily available than other Brooms. Lemon-yellow flowers on pendulous,

4- to 6-foot stems in mid-spring. Hardy in New England and similar climates. It has evergreen twig color and is equally effective in flowering time and in winter.

*C. purgans.* Provence Broom. Deep-golden flowers in spring on 3-foot evergreen stems. Hardy to Zone 6.

*C. purpureus.* Purple Broom. Low growing (up to 18 inches), and unusual for its purple flowers in mid-spring. Hardy to Zone 6.

*C. scoparius.* Scotch Broom. This is the Broom that has become naturalized over many parts of North America—in the South, at least partly through the efforts of Thomas Jefferson. Yellow flowers in mid-spring on 6-foot evergreen stems. Quite hardy (Zone 6), but parts may winterkill and leave a straggly plant. Variety ANDREANUS has flowers touched with crimson and has a more erect growing habit.

# BUNCHBERRY

TYPE Evergreen or deciduous subshrub
FAMILY *Cornaceae* (Korn-*nay*-see-ee)
GENUS *Cornus* (*Korn*-us)
SPECIES *canadensis* (kan-ad-*den*-siss)
ZONE 2

Looking like a Flowering Dogwood tree in miniature, this wild-flower is a true woody plant. It is native to mountains and open woods from Alaska and Newfoundland to West Virginia, as well as to parts of eastern Asia.

USES   In the wildflower garden or as a ground cover or a low-growing companion to Rhododendrons, Azaleas, and other plants in a naturalistic setting.

HABIT OF GROWTH   Mat-forming, with stems from 6 to 9 inches in height.

FOLIAGE   Typical Dogwood leaves, arranged on the stems in whorls, about 3 to 5 inches long, usually evergreen or semi-evergreen.

FLOWERS   The terminal clusters of inconspicuous yellow flowers are made showy by four to six large white bracts surrounding them. The flowers, which appear in May or early June, are followed by bunches of showy red berries and give this Dogwood its common name, Bunchberry.

ASSETS   An unusual, charming plant for areas in which it will thrive, with effective foliage, flowers, and fruit.

FAULTS   Bunchberry needs moist, cool, acid soil, otherwise it will languish.

CULTURE   An acid soil, rich in humus, is necessary. Light summer shade, as from Oaks, is satisfactory, although Bunchberry will take full sun if the summers remain cool and moist. This is not the easiest plant to establish, yet it is so beautiful that many gardeners feel the effort is worthwhile. One nursery that sells Bunchberry recommends planting it in a rotting log.

# BUSH CINQUEFOIL

TYPE Deciduous subshrub
FAMILY *Rosaceae* (Roh-*zay*-see-ee)
GENUS *Potentilla* (Poh-ten-*till*-uh)
SPECIES *fruticosa* (frew-tik-*koh*-suh)
ZONE 2

Bush Cinquefoil, or Shrubby Potentilla—the "shrubby" to distinguish it from non-woody plants of the genus—from China and Siberia, is winter hardy in the coldest climates. It is unpretentious, undemanding, almost everblooming.

**USES**   Plant in rock gardens or on top of rock walls or as a ground cover on sunny slopes. It can make a low, informal hedge or edging. In drifts of three or four plants it makes a pleasant flowering accent in front of taller shrubs. Plants are also suitable for a flower garden.

**HABIT OF GROWTH**   Low growing, of bushy habit; rarely over 3 feet; resembles an herbaceous perennial more than a woody plant.

**FLOWERS**   Single, Roselike flowers, about 1¼ inches across, which appear nearly continuously from summer until frost. Their most profuse display is in early summer. Color is typically a shade of yellow, but there are white varieties.

**FOLIAGE**   The leaves, Fernlike and sometimes silky in texture, are in varying shades of green.

**ASSETS**   The Bush Cinquefoil can be a lifesaver to gardeners who are tired of coping with winter injury and want flowering shrubs of easy maintenance. For color all summer, Potentilla's pretty flowers make it a worthy addition.

**FAULTS**   Under no circumstances can the Bush Cinquefoil be described as spectacular.

**CULTURE**   The plants are easy to establish in either spring or fall. They do best in full sun but will flower in light shade. They need good drainage and are even tolerant of sandy soil. When planting several, set them about a foot apart. They are easily increased by cuttings taken in early summer or by root division in fall or spring. Light pruning will make the plants grow bushier.

SPECIES AND VARIETIES *Potentilla fruticosa* is most commonly available in the following named varieties or hybrids: FARRERI, bright golden-yellow flowers from early summer to frost. Height 3–4 feet. GOLD DROP, popular variety forming a dense mound up to 2½ to 3 feet, covered all summer with golden-yellow, Buttercuplike flowers. KATHERINE DYKES, less compact in growth, with arching branches covered with yellow flowers. Height 3 feet. MOONLIGHT, paler yellow flowers. MOUNT EVEREST, outstanding white flowers that show up well against deep-green foliage.

# BUSH CLOVER

TYPE Deciduous
FAMILY *Leguminosae* (Leg-yew-min-*noh*-see)
GENUS *Lespedeza* (Les-ped-*deez*-uh)
SPECIES *Thunbergi* (*Thun*-berj-eye)
ZONE 6

A small shrub for fall color, along with Elsholtzia. The Bush Clover, an obvious member of the vast and varied Pea family, is native to Japan.

**USES** In the mixed shrub border, toward the foreground; as a single accent; or, where space permits, in groups of three. Also good against a fence or wall. An ideal use is in the background of a flower garden, especially as a background for Chrysanthemums.

**HABIT OF GROWTH** A bushy shrub up to about 4 feet, made graceful by many willowy, arching stems.

**FLOWERS** Rosy-purple Pea flowers, in dangling clusters at the ends of the branches, in early to late fall. The color is a bright one that is effective in the right setting but is not to the taste of everyone. A white form, usually listed as *L. japonica,* is considered choice, but few nurseries carry it today.

**FOLIAGE** Small, trifoliate leaves which smother the branches.

**ASSETS** Its abundant, late flowers that can blend or contrast with those of Chrysanthemums or give color to a mixed shrub planting when few other shrubs are blooming. The Bush Clover is also easy to grow and is root hardy to 20 degrees below zero.

**CULTURE** Give it a well-drained soil in full sun. It will do quite well in dry, sandy soils.

**PRUNING** In mild climates, the top growth of the Bush Clover will not die back. Even so, it is best to cut it back each spring to ground level.

# BUTTERFLY-BUSH

TYPE Deciduous
FAMILY *Loganiaceae* (Loh-gan-ee-*ay*-see-ee)
GENUS *Buddleia* (Bud-*lee*-uh)
SPECIES *alternifolia* (al-ter-nif-*foh*-lee-uh), *Davidi* (*Day*-vid-eye)
ZONE 6

Favorites of butterflies and moths are the Butterfly-bushes and this animated color they contribute to the summer garden may be the chief reason for including them. They are not really among the shrub elite even though their flowers are undeniably showy. Both the species listed here are native to China. They are also called Summer-lilac.

USES   As scattered background accents in very extensive shrubbery borders—they generally spread too much for smaller plantings—and as background for equally ambitious flower borders. (However, some varieties are more compact than others.) It is doubtful that Buddleias have sufficient all-season character to be used as solitary accents although they might be considered for placement against a sunny wall, or near a terrace where they would provide both screening and summer flowers. The flowers last well in arrangements and contribute contrast when combined with Zinnias, Petunias, and Marigolds, and other summer flowers. In fact, the Butterfly-bush is so useful as a source of cut-flower material that a hedge of different colored varieties is worth planting where space is ample.

HABIT OF GROWTH   Bushy, sometimes up to 8 feet or more and spreading as much. The Fountain Buddleia (*B. alternifolia*) has a more arching, more graceful habit than *B. Davidi* varieties. One nursery offers tree Buddleia plants, two-year-old plants which have been trained to a single stem. In very cold winters, these special plants may die back to ground level but can be retrained to the tree form.

FLOWERS   Tiny fragrant flowers arranged in terminal spires that may be 12 or more inches in length. Time of blooming is midsummer through mid-fall. Their colors range from white through pink to red and purple. The flowers of the Fountain Buddleia are arranged somewhat differently, being strung in clusters the length of the branches. They are lilac in color, also fragrant, and appear earlier, from mid-May to June.

FOLIAGE   Leaves opposite (alternate in the case of the Fountain Buddleia), long and toothed, dark green above, grayish underneath.

ASSETS   First, showy, fragrant flowers good for cutting; second, ease of growth, making them especially suitable for beginners who want to experiment with shrubs; third, ability to flower the first season in which they are planted, a factor which should appeal to the new homeowner who wants quick, temporary color before he buys better or more expensive shrubs.

FAULTS   Buddleias, with the exception of *B. alternifolia,* are die-back shrubs and contribute nothing to the landscape effect when not in flower. Some varieties of *B. Davidi* can be sprawling and even in flower not especially distinctive.

CULTURE   Buddleias need full sun and well-drained soil, and in the case of *B. Davidi* and its variants, a reasonably moist and enriched soil gives best results. When planting, add peat moss, compost, or any other organic matter on hand to soil. The Fountain Buddleia thrives in a poorer soil so long as it is well drained and is in fact considered drought resistant.

PRUNING   Treat all varieties of *B. Davidi* as die-back shrubs and cut them back to ground level every spring even if the top growth has not suffered winter injury. (However, tree-form Buddleias should not be cut to ground level unless the entire stem has died. Prune off only the part of the plant that has been winterkilled.) The new shoots that come up will be more compact and less straggly than last year's branches which have not been cut back. The Fountain Buddleia is not a die-back shrub and flowers appear on the previous year's growth, so any light pruning should be done immediately after flowering in early summer and will shape the shrub for the next year's performance.

SPECIES AND VARIETIES   *Buddleia alternifolia.* Fountain B. The choicer of the two species as far as landscape value is concerned. It can be expected to thrive where winter temperatures fall below minus 10 degrees. Its leaves are Willowlike and less coarse. Ultimate height may be 8 feet and, due to its arching branches, it needs a space of at least 12 feet in diameter.

*B. Davidi.* Butterfly-bush. Summer-lilac. Best where winter temperatures do not fall below minus 10 degrees. There are many, many named varieties and most mail-order nurseries offer several varieties. Good ones include EMPIRE BLUE; FASCINATING, lilac-pink; WHITE PROFUSION, only 3 feet tall; FORTUNE, lilac, 5 feet tall; NANHOENSIS, lavender flowers on a compact shrub, 5 feet tall; SNOWBANK, glistening white; ROYAL RED.

# CALIFORNIA-LILAC

TYPE Deciduous and evergreen
FAMILY *Rhamnaceae* (Ram-*nay*-see-ee)
GENUS *Ceanothus* (See-an-*noth*-us)
SPECIES *americanus* (am-eh-rik-*kay*-nus), *delilianus* (del-lil-ee-ay-nus), *gloriosus* (gloh-ree-*oh*-sus), *impressus* (im-*press*-us), *ovatus* (oh-*vay*-tus), *purpureus* (pur-*pew*-ree-us), *thyrsiflorus* (thir-sif-*floh*-rus)
ZONE See descriptions of species, below

California-lilac, one of the best North American natives, is almost exclusively California's, as most of the species are native there and to the Pacific Coast area. However, two species, the New Jersey-tea (*C. americanus*) and the Inland Ceanothus (*C. ovatus*), are rock-hardy and are native to the Northeast. In fact the New Jersey-tea, so named because its leaves were used as a tea substitute by the colonists during the Revolutionary War, was introduced into England in the early 1700s. Later English plant breeders used it and some of the West Coast species to produce hybrids that have become standard items in English nurseries. There has always been the hope that these beautiful blue-flowered shrubs, so handsome in California, might be grown by gardeners elsewhere. So far, such hardy hybrids have not materialized.

USES  In shrub borders or groupings; as informal hedges; as specimens and accents; against walls and fences; as ground covers, especially on dry banks and slopes.

HABIT OF GROWTH  Dense, bushy shrubs which may reach from 3 to 10 feet or with age become treelike at 25 or 30 feet. There are also prostrate and creeping species and forms that spread but never grow more than a few inches high.

FLOWERS  Small flowers in dense panicles or racemes, from ½ inch to ¾ inch in length. The clusters appear so abundantly that plants become a mass of blue. Flowering time is from early March to June.

FOLIAGE  Dark green leaves, which may be alternate or opposite, deciduous or evergreen, depending on the species. Some are glossy and spiny and resemble those of the Holly.

ASSETS  The beautiful Lilaclike flower clusters in various shades of blue and purple (rarely white), which are long lasting. Also the plant's tolerance of dry, poor soil and drought.

FAULTS  Some Ceanothuses, in particular the Point Reyes Creeper (*C. gloriosus*), are fine as ground cover where they can grow unrestrictedly but are too invasive for small areas among other plants. A few species, especially *C. thyrsiflorus,* are very susceptible to pests. Some of the best Ceanothus species cannot be tamed in the garden. Others are short-lived for no apparent reason.

CULTURE    Grow in well-drained soil in full sun. Add peat moss to the soil at planting time. Don't cultivate soil over the root area.

PRUNING    California-lilacs rarely need pruning other than that required for training for special locations. Weak shoots of the deciduous types can be removed at the base to prevent plants' becoming too tangled. Tips of all fast-growing kinds can be pinched to prevent legginess.

SPECIES AND VARIETIES    *Ceanothus americanus.* New Jersey-tea. Native from Maine to South Carolina and Texas. White flowers in short clusters from early summer until late fall. Height about 3 feet. Rarely offered by nurseries. Suitable for naturalizing in poor, stony soil in sun or semi-shade. An important species in hybridizing, despite the lowly position it occupies among flowering shrubs. Zone 4.

*C. delilianus.* Delisle Ceanothus. A hybrid of *C. americanus* and *C. coeruleus.* Light to dark blue flowers. A popular variety known in England and here is GLOIRE DE VERSAILLES, with powder-blue flowers. Zone 8.

*C. gloriosus.* Point Reyes Creeper. Native to parts of California. Prostrate plant with red branches and leathery, evergreen foliage, soft blue flower clusters. Fast-growing, useful ground cover. Zone 8.

*C. impressus.* Santa Barbara Ceanothus. Native to Southern California. Deep blue flowers in tremendous abundance in very early spring. Height about 8 feet, its branches arching and spreading to 15 feet. Zone 8.

*C. ovatus.* Inland Ceanothus. Another species found in the Northeast. Very similar to *C. americanus* but considered superior. Trouble is to find a nursery that sells it. Zone 4.

*C. purpureus.* Hollyleaf Ceanothus. Native to California. Blue-purple flower clusters and handsome evergreen foliage. Branch

color is red. Height about 4 feet. Highly recommended. Zone 7.
*C. thyrsiflorus.* Blue-blossom. Evergreen foliage and abundant blue flowers. Height up to 25 feet. Zone 8.
*C. thyrsiflorus griseus,* a variety sometimes considered another species, is considered superior. Zone 8. Hybrids or selections include REPENS, a ground cover; LOUIS EDMUNDS, with sky-blue flowers.
California nurseries list many kinds of Ceanothus. Easterners and Midwesterners who want to become acquainted with these shrubs can see a large collection at the Santa Barbara Botanic Garden.

# CAMELLIA

TYPE Evergreen
FAMILY *Theaceae* (Tee-*ay*-see-ee)
GENUS *Camellia* (Kam-*mell*-ee-yuh)
SPECIES *japonica* (jap-*pon*-ik-uh), *reticulata* (ret-ik-yew-*lay*-tuh),
*sasanqua* (sah-*san*-kwa)
ZONE 7

The lovely Camellia, so well established in parts of the South as to appear native, arrived here first with early settlers from France and England. Both *Camellia japonica,* the Common Camellia, and *C. sasanqua* are native to China and Japan; *C. reticulata* comes from China. The Camellia is a great hobby plant and there are active societies in the South and on the West Coast that are devoted to its culture.

USES  As specimen plants; as background for other, lower-growing Camellias as well as other shrubs in a border; in a foundation planting; against walls and fences, where they may or may not be trained as an espalier; as ground covers; in tubs for terrace decoration; as hedges; and as cool greenhouse plants. They make fine house plants in the North if cool, moist conditions can be supplied through the winter. Camellias are famous as corsage material, and cut sprays can be used in flower arrangements.

HABIT OF GROWTH  Sturdy, treelike growth, sometimes with two or more main stems. *C. sasanqua* is more open and spreading, and by training can be maintained at a height of 2 or 3 feet. Old plants of *C. japonica* often become trees and may reach from 20 to 40 feet in height under ideal conditions.

FLOWERS  Perhaps the most beautiful of the blooms of any flowering shrub, they have great substance whether single, semi-double, or double. They range in size from 2 to 5 inches in diameter, in color from white through pink, rose, red and variegated combinations. Camellia flowers are long lasting on the plant and when cut, and although some may appear waxy and fragile, they are amazingly tough and durable, flowering in weather that would discourage many hardier plants.

FOLIAGE  Handsome, glossy, leathery leaves, alternate and from 2 to 5 inches long, depending on species and variety. They form the perfect background for the perfect flowers.

**ASSETS**  There is no "off season" for the Camellia. In or out of bloom it is a beautiful plant. The flowers, in late fall to early spring, come when most needed. It is easy to grow.

**FAULTS**  Camellias can't be grown in most northern regions except in cool greenhouses or, with some coddling, outdoors in borderline areas.

**CULTURE**  The Camellia needs a well-drained, slightly acid, humusy soil similar to that provided for Azaleas and Rhododendrons. When planting, add a quantity of peat moss to the planting hole—about half peat moss to half soil. Maintain a mulch of leafmold and rotting leaves over the soil around the plant. If well-decayed manure is available, it can be applied. Don't cultivate around Camellia plants, as the roots are always near the surface. Cottonseed meal is a good organic fertilizer for Camellias, but it is slow to become available so must be applied before the plant needs it. Applications can be made in fall or winter. Other commercial fertilizers formulated for Camellias can be applied in spring, or just after the plant stops blooming, or according to directions on the container. Camellias thrive in regions of high humidity. Plant them in light shade; in colder regions they must be out of reach of strong, drying winds. Adequate, even moisture is essential. Camellias are grown in regions where winter temperatures rarely drop below about 10 degrees. They are common from North Carolina to Florida and along the Gulf Coast and on the West Coast from southern California north to Seattle. However, many have experimented—and successfully—with growing Camellias beyond these limits. They have thrived and bloomed for years in protected parts of New Jersey, Long Island, and Cape Cod. Out of the "Camellia Belt," plants must be protected from vicious winter winds with burlap screens, polyethylene tents, or cut evergreens.

**PRUNING**  Depends on plant shape, degree of growth, and use to which plant is being put. Some plants need little care other than removal of faded flowers. Any necessary pruning can be done while plants are flowering or just after flowers have faded.

**PESTS AND DISEASES**  Although the Camellia may be attacked by any of an impressive array of pests and diseases, the home gardener with a few plants is not likely to have much trouble. *Mealybugs* may be controlled by a spray containing malathion. The *black vine weevil* may chew on the leaves, leaving characteristic uneven holes. Spray the lower parts of the plants and the soil surface with dieldrin or chlordane in spring, following manufacturer's directions. *Chlorosis* of leaves (uneven yellow spots) may indicate a need for iron chelates (Sequestrene or an equivalent product).

**SPECIES AND VARIETIES**  *Camellia japonica,* Common Camellia. There are hundreds of varieties originating from this species, a rugged, treelike shrub with evergreen leaves about 4 inches long. Varieties bloom over a season lasting from October to April. Consult catalogues of specialists for names and descriptions.

*C. reticulata.* This Chinese species, introduced later than other species, is more tender than they; it is lanky, its foliage dull. Its flowers are large and handsome, but *C. reticulata* and its varieties are mainly grown in greenhouses.

*C. sasanqua.* Beautiful and desirable, with hundreds of varieties. A useful, versatile landscaping plant, perhaps slightly more tolerant of full sun and cold than the Common Camellia.

# CHERRY-LAUREL

TYPE Evergreen
FAMILY *Rosaceae* (Roh-*zay*-see-ee)
GENUS *Prunus* (*Proon*-us)
SPECIES *caroliniana* (kar-rol-in-ee-*ay*-nuh), *laurocerasus* (law-roh-ser-*ras*-us)
ZONE 6, 7

Ruggedly handsome are the Cherry-laurels, and in fact their leathery leaves in winter can outshine those of most Rhododendrons, which must curl and droop to survive low temperatures. The Carolina Cherry-laurel (*Prunus caroliniana*) is native in coastal areas from North Carolina to Texas; the common Cherry-laurel (*P. laurocerasus*) is native to parts of southeastern Europe.

USES    As hedges and windbreaks, especially in the South and on the West Coast; farther north, in foundation plantings, as specimen plants in a shrub border, or as occasional accents against walls or fences. The Cherry-laurel is most amenable to shearing, and for this reason it is commonly used in tubs and planters for terrace decoration, where it can be kept espaliered or rounded or trimmed to other exotic shapes.

HABIT OF GROWTH    Broad, upright, quick-growing; rounded if not pruned otherwise. Height from 6 to 18 feet, depending on climate and training.

FLOWERS    White, fragrant, about ⅓ inch across, in racemes 2 to 5 inches long, in mid-spring; purple-black cherries follow to make a rather showy display in late summer.

FOLIAGE    Outstanding. Long, evergreen, very lustrous leaves with serrated edges.

ASSETS    Foliage; the fragrant flower spikes, which show up well; the character of the plant which, where hardy, can adapt to a number of landscaping uses. The Cherry-laurels are very fast growing.

FAULTS    Their use is restricted to the mild-climate areas of the West Coast and the South, and, in the East, to Long Island and comparable areas. (See below for two varieties hardy to 10 degrees below zero.) Where the Cherry-laurel thrives, it should not be planted too close to shallow-rooted plants from which it can steal moisture and nourishment.

CULTURE   Plant in moderately rich soil which is well drained, in full sun or light shade. In the North, in borderline areas of hardiness, place the Cherry-laurel in a protected site.

PRUNING   Trimming or shearing can be done at the convenience of the gardener, the degree depending on the purpose for which the plant is being grown.

SPECIES AND VARIETIES   *Prunus caroliniana* (sometimes listed as *Laurocerasus caroliniana*). Carolina Cherry-laurel, Wild-orange, Mock-orange. Creamy-white flowers. Zone 7.
*P. laurocerasus* (sometimes listed as *Laurocerasus officinalis*). The common Cherry-laurel. Zones 6 and 7. Its variety SCHIP-KAENSIS is considered hardy to 10 degrees below zero. The variety ZABELIANA, of the same hardiness, grows to between 6 and 8 feet tall.

# *CHINESE REDBUD*

TYPE Deciduous
FAMILY *Leguminosae* (Leg-yew-min-*noh*-see)
GENUS *Cercis* (*Ser*-siss)
SPECIES *chinensis* (chin-*nen*-siss)
ZONE 6

Capable of one of the gaudiest floral effects of spring, the Chinese Redbud makes a large tree in its native China, more often a low or medium-sized shrub in this country. It is sometimes called Judas-tree.

USES   It needs careful placement, as the strong magenta flowers may clash with other spring-flowering material and certain house-paint colors. Otherwise it can be used in mixed shrub borders, as a specimen, and as a bushy companion to the white Flowering Dogwood (*Cornus florida*). Its branches can be forced into flower in late winter and are effective in arrangements.

HABIT OF GROWTH   Many-stemmed, upright, varying from a dense vase shape to an open, even straggly, form. It may reach 12 feet or so in protected, less rugged northern areas, but usually it remains at 8 feet or less.

FLOWERS   Deep rosy-purple Pea flowers, ½ inch long, in dense clusters all along the branches, before the leaves open.

FOLIAGE   Shiny, deep-green leaves, heart-shaped.

ASSETS   A showy shrub which starts to flower while young and which can be spectacular in the right setting—say, contrasted with white Tulips—or even as an adjunct to a white house or against a white wall or fence.

FAULTS   Its strong color, which may clash with other plants; its susceptibility to extreme winter temperatures; and its fussiness about transplanting.

CULTURE   The Chinese Redbud should be planted or moved only in the spring, and when it is beyond the seedling stage it should be moved only with a ball of earth enclosing its roots. It needs full sun and an average, well-drained soil. Once established it requires no special care beyond pruning back top growth that may have been injured by severe winter cold.

# *CORNELIAN-CHERRY*

TYPE Deciduous
FAMILY *Cornaceae* (Korn-*nay*-see-ee)
GENUS *Cornus* (*Korn*-us)
SPECIES *mas* (mass), *officinalis* (off-iss-in-*nay*-liss)
ZONE 5

Not a Cherry at all but a Dogwood, and one of the first shrubs of spring to make a substantial show. Neither species is native to this country.

USES    In naturalistic or woodland situations, as background shrubs in mixed borders, as hedges, or as specimens. The branches can be cut in winter, brought indoors and forced into flower. Whether forced or cut from the shrubs while in full bloom, the branches are excellent in arrangements; the Cornelian-cherry is worth growing for this purpose alone.

HABIT OF GROWTH    Large bushy shrubs, multi-stemmed unless trained otherwise; may eventually reach 20 feet or more.

FLOWERS    Unlike those of the Flowering Dogwood tree (*Cornus florida*) in that they are not surrounded by white bracts, they are bright yellow, small, and carried in tight clusters along the branches in late March or early April, before the leaves appear. The effect is a haze of gold all over the plant, very effective in a landscape that is barely beginning to awaken. The flowers are followed by edible, scarlet, Plumlike fruits which the birds like.

FOLIAGE    Shiny green leaves, opposite, about 4½ inches long, which take on reddish or yellow tints late in fall.

ASSETS    The very early flowers, hardiness (to 20 degrees below zero), dense, attractive foliage which gives autumn color, and general adaptability to many landscape uses.

FAULTS    These shrubs are too large for small properties.

CULTURE    Easy-to-grow shrubs in average, well-drained soils; adaptable to full sun or light shade.

PRUNING    None necessary, although it is possible to make a small tree of the Cornelian-cherry by removing all stems except one.

SPECIES *Cornus mas*. Cornelian-cherry. Native to southern Europe and parts of the Orient. There is a variety with creamy-white and red leaves.

*C. officinalis*. Cornelian-cherry. Native to China and Japan. Differs from *C. mas* in having peeling bark, which is interesting in winter, and in being slightly earlier flowering.

# COTONEASTER

TYPE Deciduous and evergreen
FAMILY *Rosaceae* (Roz-*ay*-see-ee)
GENUS *Cotoneaster* (Kot-toh-nee-*ass*-ter)
SPECIES *dielsiana* (deel-see-*ay*-nuh), *floribunda* (floh-rib-*bund*-uh), *hupehensis* (hoo-pay-*en*-siss), *multiflora* (mull-tif-*floh*-ruh), *racemiflora* (ras-em-if-*floh*-ruh), *rosea* (*roh*-zee-uh), *salicifolia* (sal-iss-if-*foh*-lee-uh)
ZONE 4, 5, 6

It may be debatable whether the flowers of Cotoneaster are showy enough to put it in the class of a flowering shrub. The kinds included here do have prominent flowers, however, and there is no question as to the value of the vivid berries that follow. No Cotoneasters are native to the United States.

USES  Cotoneasters are most versatile, being suited to shrub-border or specimen use (especially the species listed above); others are excellent for banks or slopes, or against walls or fences. The shrubby kinds can be used for hedges along boundaries, or can be situated in semi-naturalistic areas. The low-growing, evergreen Cotoneasters make attractive ground covers. The fruits are attractive to birds.

HABIT OF GROWTH  Cotoneasters differ tremendously in habit, some being low-growing, even ground hugging, while others have graceful, upright growth with branches slightly arching.

FLOWERS  Clusters of small white or pink flowers in mid- or late spring, showy because of their abundance. The bright berries that follow are prized more than the flowers.

FOLIAGE  Deciduous, semi-evergreen or evergreen leaves (depending upon species), alternate, and often especially handsome. The fall coloring of some is distinctive.

ASSETS  The abundance of flowers as well as fruit (attractive to birds), handsome foliage, and general variation and versatility of the many species. Some are exceptionally hardy; others are best in mild climates. Only a few have been considered here.

FAULTS  From the point of view of flower effect alone, there are better shrubs, but to counter this there is their long-lasting bright fruit.

CULTURE  Grow in well-drained, average soil in full sun. Very light, high shade is satisfactory. Cotoneasters are considered hard to transplant, although young plants in peat pots or older ones, container-grown, now offered by many nurseries, are not difficult to establish. Older plants are best set out in spring. Pruning to shape plants may be done after flowering.

PESTS AND DISEASES The home gardener will encounter few. *Red spider* may be found, especially when plants are crowded, are being grown in light shade, and with poor circulation of air. Use any modern all-purpose spray that contains malathion. Occasionally hose off the foliage forcefully. *Scale,* including *San Jose* and *oyster-shell,* may occur. Spray with dormant strength lime-sulphur in early spring; with malathion in late spring.

SPECIES AND VARIETIES *Cotoneaster dielsiana.* Deciduous shrub, to 8 feet, with arching branches. Small, pink flowers stud the branches, to be followed by scarlet berries in the fall; the berries are attractive to pheasants and other birds. Foliage may turn orange in fall. Hardy to Zone 5 (20 degrees below zero). *C. floribunda* (botanically *C. bullata floribunda*). Deciduous, bushy, with arching branches. Foliage blue-green. Flowers profuse, followed by bright red fruit. Hardy to 20 degrees below zero.
*C. hupehensis.* Graceful, deciduous shrub to 6 feet, with white flowers conspicuous in mid-spring all along the branches. Large red fruits in August. Foliage turns orange and red in fall.
*C. multiflora.* Deciduous, graceful shrub with arching branches; to 10 feet; in late May, covered with clusters of white flowers similar to those of the Hawthorn. Long-lasting bright red berries follow. Foliage is blue-green. Very hardy.
*C. racemiflora.* Deciduous, spreading shrub to 7 feet, with large white flower clusters followed by long-lasting red fruits. Hardy to 20 degrees below zero.
*C. rosea.* Deciduous shrub to 7 feet, its branches covered with pink flower clusters in mid-spring; red fruit. Blue-green leaves which take on autumn coloration. Very hardy.
*C. salicifolia.* Willowleaf Cotoneaster. Deciduous, to 10 feet; evergreen in mild climates. Snowy white flower clusters in late May, followed by bright red fruits. Attractive leaves turn purple-red in fall. Considered choice. Hardy to zero.

# CRAPE-MYRTLE

TYPE Deciduous
FAMILY *Lythraceae* (Lith-*ray*-see-ee)
GENUS *Lagerstroemia* (Lay-jer-*streem*-ee-uh)
SPECIES *indica* (*inn*-dik-uh)
ZONE 7

This showy, summer-blooming shrub so prevalent in Florida and other mild-climate areas is root hardy as far north as mild parts of Massachusetts and top hardy to central Missouri and comparable climates. The Crape-myrtle is not native to the South—it came from China.

USES   In the South it may serve as a flowering tree or as a large shrub in a variety of situations. In the North it has been popular as a tub plant in cool greenhouses. More recently it has been offered to northern gardeners as a die-back shrub, as its roots will survive freezing temperatures after top growth is killed. New growth appears each spring. Thus it may be used in the background of flower gardens, in the foreground of mixed shrub borders, or as a tub plant on terraces.

HABIT OF GROWTH   A tree or large shrub in the South and in mild sections of the West Coast. Elsewhere it may reach 3 to 4 feet, dying back to ground level each winter.

FLOWERS   Fringed flowers with crinkly, crepey texture, carried in large, showy clusters often 8 inches long, in summer. Colors include pink, rosy-red, purple, and white.

FOLIAGE   Leaves, opposite, are 2 to 3 inches long.

ASSETS   Its showy flowers and attractive foliage.

FAULTS   Lack of positive hardiness for the Northerner.

CULTURE   Grow in full sun, in well-drained average soil. In the North, give a protected situation.

PRUNING   Crape-myrtle blooms on new wood, so pruning, if necessary, can be done in spring. In the North, plants are self-pruning, the top growth dying back to the ground each winter. Elsewhere, prune as necessary to shape.

VARIETIES   There are many varieties offered by nurseries. Of special interest are new dwarf and semi-dwarf varieties such as SNOW BABY, height 3 to 4 feet; LOW FLAME, brilliant red flowers, height 4 to 5 feet; BLUE MIDGET, soft lavender flowers, plant 4 to 5 feet in height.

# CUT-LEAF STEPHANANDRA

TYPE Deciduous
FAMILY *Rosaceae* (Roz-*ay*-see-ee)
GENUS *Stephanandra* (Steff-en-*and*-ruh)
SPECIES *incisa* (in-*sye*-suh)
ZONE 5

The Cut-leaf Stephanandra always wins praise for its foliage and amiable habit of growth, but it scores less favorably for its flowers. Nevertheless it *is* a flowering shrub, the flowers dainty but still effective. It is native to Japan and Korea.

HABIT OF GROWTH    Graceful, arching branches, slender, irregular, and reddish-brown, to about 5 feet; eventually forms a round, dense shrub. A dwarf variety CRISPA NANA grows about 2 feet high, spreading to about 3 feet across.

USES    Pretty and substantial enough to use as a specimen in front of taller shrubs in a mixed border or corner grouping. The dwarf form (CRISPA NANA) makes an excellent ground cover for a variety of situations, as it grows only 2 feet high. The airy flowers and foliage can be effective in arrangements.

FLOWERS    Small, starlike flowers, greenish-white, in feathery panicles at the ends of shoots in late spring (mid-June).

FOLIAGE    Alternate leaves, about 2½ inches long, deeply cut and giving a Fernlike and lacy pattern that is most desirable. Color varies from bronze-green in spring and summer to red and copper shades in the fall.

ASSETS    An easy-to-grow shrub, with excellent foliage and a pleasing growth habit, interesting the year around in the garden. Attractive even in winter, when the bright brown tint of its twigs and branches is especially apparent.

FAULTS    A shrub that seems to be going out of fashion. It is hard to find in nurseries except for its dwarf form. Its flowers are too subtle to put it among the elite of flowering shrubs.

CULTURE    It grows in average, well-drained soil. Very sandy or clay soils should have organic material, such as peat moss, added at planting time. Best foliage color is developed in full sun, but light shade is also tolerated.

PRUNING Some top growth may be winterkilled, in which case cut back to live in spring. After flowering, some branches may be thinned out, either by removing them at the ground level or by cutting back to a side branch. Stephanandra is very responsive to pruning and is easily kept shapely and neat.

# DAPHNE

TYPE Deciduous and evergreen
FAMILY *Thymelaeaceae* (Tye-me-lye-*ay*-see-ee)
GENUS *Daphne* (*Daff*-nee)
SPECIES *Burkwoodi* (*Burk*-wood-eye), *cneorum* (nee-*ohr*-um), *genkwa* (*genk*-wah), *mezereum* (me-*zer*-ree-um), *odora* (oh-*doh*-ruh)
ZONE See descriptions of species, below

Daphne, to most gardeners, evokes the memory of fragrance. These shrubs are native to Asia and Europe.

USES  Best for occasional use in the foreground of a mixed shrub planting, as they do not contribute special landscaping value except for Garland-flower (*Daphne cneorum*) illustrated, a showy plant in the rock garden or as an edging to a flower border. They are also suitable for an open woodland along a path or in the foreground of a small shrub grouping where their flowers can be enjoyed (and smelled) at close range. Its flowers are illustrated here. February Daphne (*Daphne mezereum*) is ideal for early forcing. In fact it is worthwhile to grow several plants for this purpose alone.

HABIT OF GROWTH  Upright, rather stiff shrubs to 3 or 4 feet, although the Garland-flower (illustrated) forms a low, mounded, and trailing shrub to 12 inches.

FLOWERS  Usually very sweetly fragrant flowers, small and star-shaped, in clusters strung tight against the stems. Colors include reddish-purple, pink, lilac, and white. The Garland-flower carries its bright pink flowers in rounded clusters at the ends of its branches. The berries that follow on some species are prominent.

FOLIAGE  Opposite or alternate, deciduous or evergreen, depending upon the species; leaves 1–4 inches long. The evergreen foliage of the Garland-flower is the most effective.

ASSETS  The fragrance of most species, as well as the unexpected delight of having their flowers so early in the spring. The flowers of the Somerset Daphne (*Daphne Burkwoodi*) and of Garland-flower are especially showy and fragrant.

FAULTS  Daphnes are considered short-lived when compared with most shrubs, although experience on this score varies. They are also considered difficult to grow.

CULTURE Daphnes are difficult to transplant. Most nursery-men offer young, pot- or container-grown material, although plants with a substantial root ball ("balled and burlapped") are sometimes found. A well-drained soil is essential, but it should contain enough humus so that it does not become bone dry. Daphnes apparently prefer an alkaline soil—especially the February Daphne, *D. mezereum*—and should therefore be expected to thrive in soil prepared for Lilacs. Full sun is best, especially for the Garland-flower, but the others can take some light or open shade. Pruning is essential only for the removal of dead stems.

SPECIES *Daphne Burkwoodi*. Somerset Daphne. (Hybrid of *D. caucasica* and *D. cneorum;* originated in England.) Very fragrant and showy pale-pink flowers in late spring. Dark-green leaves, evergreen in mild areas. Height 4 to 5 feet. Very hardy.

*D. cneorum*. Garland-flower. Rose Daphne. Very fragrant, bright-pink flowers in mid-spring. Attractive evergreen leaves on low-growing plants to 10 or 12 inches. Hardy to Zone 5, and very choice.

*D. genkwa*. Lilac Daphne. Violet-blue flowers on arching, leaf-less branches in early spring. A lovely little shrub but considered temperamental. Should endure winter temperatures of 10 degrees below zero (Zone 5), but stems sometimes winterkill; when this happens, cutting them off at ground level may force new growth. Needs slightly alkaline soil.

*D. mezereum*. February Daphne. The common name is misleading except in the South, as this Daphne blooms in April in the North. However, its bud-crowded stems quickly burst into flower when they are brought indoors during the winter. Purple-red flowers, about ¼ inch across, with spicy, faint fragrance, before the foliage appears. Height 3 feet. Needs alkaline soil. There is a rare white form. Zone 5.

*D. odora*. Winter Daphne. Very fragrant, small rose-purple flowers in early spring. Difficult to establish; when this has been accomplished, it shouldn't be moved or cultivated. Best in the upper South or where temperatures do not drop below about 10 degrees (Zone 7). There is some evidence that it is tolerant of acid soil.

# *DEUTZIA*

TYPE Deciduous
FAMILY *Saxifragaceae* (Sax-iff-ruh-*gay*-see-ee)
GENUS *Deutzia* (*Dewt*-see-uh)
SPECIES *elegantissima* (el-eg-an-*tiss*-im-uh), *gracilis* (*grass*-il-iss), *kalmiaeflora* (kal-mih-ee-*floh*-ruh), *Lemoinei* (Lem-*moyn*-ee), *scabra* (*skay*-bruh)
ZONE See descriptions of species, below

"Prettiness" perhaps best describes the flowers of the Deutzia. The species are native to Asia, but most of the varieties and hybrids grown today were developed in France many years ago.

USES    As filler material wherever their late-spring flowers can be enjoyed most effectively—such as in a mixed shrub border, as background to a flower garden to contrast with late-blooming Tulips, or, in the case of the low-growing, compact kinds, as a low hedge around a terrace, entrance or walk. They make excellent cutting material for flower arrangers.

HABIT OF GROWTH    Upright, many-stemmed shrubs varying in height from 3 to 10 feet, rather graceful when blooms arch their branches.

FLOWERS    An abundance of fluffy white, pink, or pink-tinted flowers, about 1 inch across, in racemes or panicles in late spring.

FOLIAGE    Opposite, pale-green leaves of no special distinction.

ASSETS    Their long-lasting flowers, which make the bushes into bouquets of bloom. The low-growing *Deutzia gracilis,* with its pure-white or pink flowers, is the most distinctive; it is especially useful for small gardens, as it will not outgrow its space.

FAULTS    After flowering, the Deutzias have no eye appeal.

CULTURE    Full sun or light, high shade, and well-drained soil that can retain moisture during dry periods. They are free from diseases and insects.

PRUNING    Occasionally some of the newer stems partially winterkill, in which case they should be cut back to live wood in early spring. Immediately after flowering, old stems can be cut out at the base to keep the shrubs open and to stimulate new shoot growth. Deutzias generally need annual pruning directly after flowering to keep them flowering abundantly.

SPECIES AND VARIETIES   *Deutzia elegantissima.* A hybrid, 4 to 5 feet in height, with rose-pink flowers, slightly fragrant. Hardy to 10 degrees below zero. Zone 6.

*D. gracilis.* Slender Deutzia. By far the best available Deutzia. Neat and compact shrub, to 2½–4 feet, with racemes of pure-white or pink flowers in late May. Hardy to 20 degrees below zero (Zone 5). This shrub is so effective in flower that the home gardener can find many uses for it; it is easy to increase by lifting the clump in early fall and pulling it apart.

*D. kalmiaeflora.* Hybrid with pale-pink flowers reminiscent of those of Mountain-laurel (*Kalmia*). It does not grow over 3 feet high and should be useful in small gardens. Hardy to 20 degrees below zero. Zone 5.

*D. Lemoinei.* Tall-growing hybrid (to 7 feet) with white flowers. Very hardy. There are lower-growing, more compact forms such as *D. Lemoinei compacta.* Hardy to protected areas of Zone 4.

*D. scabra* (often listed as *D. crenata*). Tall-growing, to 8 feet, with white or rose-tinged flowers, single or double, in late spring. PRIDE OF ROCHESTER has double white flowers. Hardy to Zone 5 (20 degrees below zero).

# DUSTY ZENOBIA

TYPE Deciduous or semi-evergreen
FAMILY *Ericaceae* (Ehr-ik-*ay*-see-ee)
GENUS *Zenobia* (Zen-*noh*-bee-uh)
SPECIES *pulverulenta* (pull-ver-oo-*lent*-uh)
ZONE 6

Yet another member of the Heath family, this shrub is native from North Carolina to northern Florida. Its flowers are more similar to those of Andromeda, Blueberry, and Heath (*Erica*) than to those of Azalea or Rhododendron, which are in the same family.

USES    As companion plants to other shrubs in the same family. It is interesting in the foreground of Rhododendron groupings or colonized in light shade, especially in naturalistic situations.

HABIT OF GROWTH    An informal, upright shrub to 3 or 4 feet (it may reach 6 feet under ideal conditions, but slowly), with branches eventually arching. It will form colonies, spreading by layers.

FLOWERS    White, bell-shaped, about ½ inch across, in clusters on racemes at the ends of the branches. Their effect is that of a larger Lily-of-the-valley, with a slight aniselike scent. Blooming time is late spring (May to early June).

FOLIAGE    The leaves, responsible for the "dusty" in Zenobia's common name, are oval or oblong, alternate, and about 3 inches long. They are grayish and covered with a bluish bloom. The variety *nuda* lacks this coating and is not as attractive.

ASSETS    Attractive flowers and foliage as well as hardiness make this plant desirable for those interested in the Heath family.

FAULTS    Dusty Zenobia needs acid soil. It is not carried by many nurseries.

CULTURE    Grows easily in light shade in an acid soil, on the sandy side, that is full of peat. In other soils than acid ones, add a quantity of peat moss to the planting holes.

# *ELSHOLTZIA*

TYPE Deciduous
FAMILY *Labiatae* (Lah-bee-*ay*-tee)
GENUS *Elsholtzia* (El-*sholt*-see-uh)
SPECIES *Stauntoni* (*Staun*-ton-eye)
ZONE 6

This plant's name may be a mouthful to say (it has no common name except the dubious one of Mint-shrub), but it does commemorate a German physician and botanist, J. S. Elsholtz. It is a member of the Mint family and comes from northern China.

USES   A shrub for autumn, of such stature that it might be massed with certain Chrysanthemums for a dramatic effect, or grouped in the foreground of a mixed shrub border for late color.

HABIT OF GROWTH   Semi-woody or die-back shrub, to 2 or 3 feet, in areas with comparable climates to that of the New York City region; reaches 3 to 5 feet in mild climates.

FLOWERS   Eight-inch, one-sided spikes of lipped lavender-pink flowers in late September and early October.

FOLIAGE   Pale green, 5-inch leaves that are aromatic.

ASSETS   Its spikes of long-lasting flowers late in the season.

FAULTS   It is of no value except for its autumnal flowers.

CULTURE   Easy to grow in average, well-drained soil in full sun. Even when the full top growth is not killed back by winter, it is best to cut back the entire plant at ground level in the spring to avoid a gawky, uneven form.

# *ENKIANTHUS*

TYPE Deciduous
FAMILY *Ericaceae* (Ehr-ik-*ay*-see-ee)
GENUS *Enkianthus* (En-kee-*anth*-us)
SPECIES *campanulatus* (kam-pan-yew-*lay*-tus), *cernuus* (*ser*-new-us), *perulatus* (per-yew-*lay*-tus)
ZONE 5

A gem of a flowering shrub is the Enkianthus, a gift to Western gardeners from Japan.

USES   Use it as a tall accent in a foundation planting; against walls and fences; in any grouping of Azaleas and Rhododendrons; or in the background of a mixed shrub border.

HABIT OF GROWTH   Always graceful and distinctive, the Enkianthus somewhat resembles some deciduous Azaleas, its branches growing upward in whorls or tiers. The species listed here range in height from 6 to 12 feet.

FLOWERS   Clusters of dangling bells, about ½ inch long, in May, often before the leaves are fully developed. These pale yellow flowers are brightened by contrasting stripes of red or brown and, while they do not make the showiest of spring displays, their charm cannot be questioned.

FOLIAGE   Attractive alternate, toothed leaves which appear to be slightly waxy. They offer a bonus by turning brilliant red and orange in the autumn.

ASSETS   Refinement in all its parts. Neat yet distinctive growth habits, interesting flowers, fine foliage, and winter hardiness. It makes a fine companion to other acid-soil shrubs, complementing them yet at the same time offering contrast.

CULTURE   Enkianthus must have an acid soil, the same as is needed by Mountain-laurel, Azalea, and Rhododendron, preferably in the form of a sandy loam with ample quantities of peat moss added. It will grow in light shade or full sun. As with Azaleas and Rhododendrons, it needs a good soaking during droughts. Mulch with leafmold, decaying Oak leaves, or wood chips. Enkianthus can be easily grown from seed by the home gardener. Sprinkle the fine seed on a bed of sphagnum moss, previously soaked and then drained, in a container which can be kept moist by a tent of polyethylene. If the seeds are started in early winter indoors, they will germinate in a few weeks, grow rapidly and can be shifted in early spring into a flat of equal parts of peat moss, sand, and soil. When the weather has warmed and frost danger has passed, the young seedlings can be set out in rows in the home nursery where, under lath shade, they grow rapidly the first summer. Enkianthus rarely needs pruning.

SPECIES  *Enkianthus campanulatus.* Redvein Enkianthus. The most available Enkianthus, although still unknown to many nurserymen and shrub lovers. Grows to 20 or more feet in the wild, but is more likely to remain around 6 to 8 feet in the home garden. It is sometimes possible to find variations with paler or brighter flowers. The flowers are delicately striped, giving the plant its name "redvein."

*E. cernuus.* Very similar to *E. campanulatus,* with flowers ranging from white to bright red.

*E. perulatus.* White flowers and scarlet fall foliage.

# *FALSE-SPIREA*

TYPE Deciduous
FAMILY *Rosaceae* (Roz-*ay*-see-ee)
GENUS *Sorbaria* (Sor-*bay*-ree-uh)
SPECIES *Aitchisoni* (*At*-key-son-ee), *sorbifolia* (sorb-if-*foh*-lee-uh)
ZONE 5

These are pretty yet not well-known shrubs—of interest to the person especially interested in flowering shrubs, and worthwhile for those with large properties, perhaps of less value to gardeners with small places. The False-spireas, closely related to Spirea and to Ocean Spray, are from Asia.

USES    Best in colonies where the mass effect of their flowers can be appreciated, such as at the edge of a lawn expanse or naturalized in front of strong evergreens such as Pines or Hemlocks; or use sparingly in large shrub borders.

HABIT OF GROWTH    Graceful and upright until flower panicles arch the stems. Ultimate height from 4 to 8 feet. *Sorbaria sorbifolia* spreads quickly because of its suckering habit, but all species sucker to some degree.

FLOWERS    Effective panicles of small, white flowers, ¼ inch across. The panicles vary from 12 to 18 inches long and appear from early summer to early fall.

FOLIAGE    Fernlike, pinnate leaves consisting of many leaflets about ½ inch wide; bright green. They resemble those of the Mountain-ash and appear especially early in spring.

ASSETS    Definitely worthwhile for mass planting, especially in informal naturalistic settings and as a flowering accent against evergreens. The flowers can be most dramatic in summer, and the shrub's habit is generally pleasing, both in foliage characteristics and shape. False-spireas are comparatively hardy and easy to grow.

FAULTS    All species of False-spirea tend to sucker, some more than others; for this reason these shrubs are not for small properties.

CULTURE    They are tolerant of poor soil but grow best and spread fastest in average, moist, rich soil. Full sun or light shade is suitable. Easy to increase because of their suckers, which can be severed from the main plant.

PRUNING  In colder areas, False-spireas are best grown as die-back shrubs, with the top growth cut off at ground level each spring. The resulting stems, which may make 4 to 5 feet of growth, will bear flowers that summer. In milder areas, or protected areas in cold zones, some removal of stems should be practiced every few years to force strong new growth. The flower panicles, after flowering, droop dejectedly on the shrub and, if possible, it is best to remove them.

SPECIES  *Sorbaria Aitchisoni.* Kashmir False-spirea. An attractive species, hardy to 5 degrees below zero, although the top growth may winterkill. Ultimate height is about 9 feet unless annual cutting back of stems to ground level keeps growth lower. Attractive bright-green leaflets on red petioles, with flower panicles also carried on red stems, increase this shrub's appeal. It blooms in midsummer.

*S. sorbifolia.* Ural False-spirea. Considered less desirable than the preceding species, because of its very pronounced suckering habit; it is nevertheless useful for landscaping larger properties. Its soft stems are green and pithy, its flower panicles more narrow than those of *S. Aitchisoni* and appear earlier, usually starting in June. Its height is from 3 to 6 feet.

# *FIRETHORN*

TYPE Evergreen, semi-evergreen, or deciduous
FAMILY *Rosaceae* (Roz-*ay*-see-ee)
GENUS *Pyracantha* (Pye-ruh-*kanth*-uh)
SPECIES *coccinea* (kok-*sin*-ee-uh)
ZONE 6

While the Firethorn's full glory comes when its berries turn orange-red in the fall, its clusters of white flowers in the spring can be showy enough for it to be counted as a bona-fide flowering shrub. The Firethorn, which is closely related to the Hawthorn, is native to parts of southern Europe and Asia. Gardeners in the South and on the West Coast can grow several species and varieties that are not hardy in most of the North.

USES  A versatile shrub that has many uses, provided the gardener is willing to take time to train and prune its fast-growing branches. It is useful in foundation plantings, especially of contemporary homes with stark lines; against walls and fences; and as a specimen in a variety of situations. Where there is space, it can make an attractive hedge. It is often listed as a "vine" because of its long branches, which can make tremendous growth in a season or two and which can be trained as one would a vine.

HABIT OF GROWTH  A Firethorn unrestricted by pruning makes a rounded, wide-spreading, many-stemmed plant to 12 feet. Thorns or spines, about ½ inch long, are scattered along the branches. Trained plants, either as specimens or in hedges, can be kept as low as 4 feet.

FLOWERS  Flat-topped clusters of small white flowers, each ⅓ inch across, in late spring; produced in such abundance as to be effective. The berries which follow the flowers turn bright orange or red, and in fall they really light up the bush. Birds like the berries, but they do not usually devour them overnight, so this fruit display often lasts well into fall.

FOLIAGE  Evergreen, semi-evergreen, or deciduous leaves, alternate and finely toothed, about 1½ inches long. Both flowers and fruit show well against the shining, dark-green foliage, which can be quite dense, especially on bushes kept compact by annual pruning. Winter coloring of leaves is purple. When the leaves are damaged by winter burn—often the case in the North—new ones appear to replenish the branches in the spring.

ASSETS   Firethorn's late-spring flowers, its bright berry display in the fall, and the generally graceful and distinctive plant habit, amenable to various uses and training. Also its fast growth (especially desirable for impatient new home owners), and its tolerance of lean, dry soil.

FAULTS   Firethorn can grow rampantly, and young plants can too quickly outgrow their location. Training and restrictive pruning are almost a must for Firethorn unless it is placed in the open with no space limitations. Established plants are difficult to transplant. Nurseries usually offer young plants in containers, which suffer little transplanting setback.

CULTURE   Firethorn likes full sun, but will grow in light shade, in average, well-drained soil. It is also tolerant of sandy, dry soils.

PRUNING   Degree and type of pruning depend on use to which bush has been put. For a hedge, it can be clipped so that subsequent growth will be twiggy, with dense foliage. Or a hedge, if there is space enough, can be allowed to grow naturally, in which case branches will assume a graceful, arching habit. Prune at any time.

VARIETIES   There are many varieties of *Pyracantha coccinea,* perhaps the most widely distributed being LALANDI. It has a yellow-fruited variety. KASAN is considered very hardy and is recommended for areas where temperatures may fall to 20 degrees below zero. LOWBOY forms a broad, dense bush and remains about 6 feet high. WYATTI is also hardy, with a dense, spreading habit.

# *FLOWERING ALMOND*

TYPE Deciduous
FAMILY *Rosaceae* (Roz-*ay*-see-ee)
GENUS *Prunus* (*Proon*-us)
SPECIES *glandulosa* (glan-dew-*loh*-suh)
ZONE 5

Most of the flowering fruits are considered trees but a few, including this Flowering Almond, have the form and characteristics of shrubs. Native to China and Japan, this species has long been known here; it is one of the plants that would fit into an old-fashioned dooryard garden. (Some other plants in the same genus—for example, *Prunus triloba,* described in the section on Flowering Plum—are also called "Flowering Almond.")

USES   Strictly for its pretty spring flowers, which can be effective among spring bulbs and which show up well in the foreground of mixed shrub plantings or even as early accents in flower borders. It can be planted against walls and fences and even espaliered.

HABIT OF GROWTH   Low-growing plants, to about 4 feet, with branches slender, upright then slightly arching.

FLOWERS   They are double, white or pink, and grow close to the branches from top to bottom; they appear in late April or early May. The blooms look like fluffy, feathery balls and usually hide the stems completely, giving the plant a quaint prettiness. The fruits that follow in summer are cherries (not almonds!), about ⅓ inch in diameter.

FOLIAGE   Alternate, satiny green leaves after the flowers.

ASSETS   Great hardiness—Flowering Almond easily endures winter temperatures to 20 degrees below zero—and showy spring flowers.

FAULTS   Not for gardeners who value shrubs beyond their floral contribution.

CULTURE   Easy to grow in full sun in average, well-drained soil. If plants have been grafted on a different stock, care is necessary to prevent unwanted growth of the root stock from enveloping the Almond.

PRUNING Cut off any shoots that come from understock if the Flowering Almond is a grafted rather than own-root plant. Flowers are produced on young wood, so pruning after the flowers have faded can be done to shape the plants when necessary. Occasionally, full stems can be removed to stimulate new growth to maintain the plant's vitality.

# *FLOWERING CHERRY*

TYPE Deciduous
FAMILY *Rosaceae* (Roz-*ay*-see-ee)
GENUS *Prunus* (*Proon*-us)
SPECIES *subhirtella* (sub-her-*tell*-uh), *tomentosa* (toh-men-*toh*-suh)
ZONE 3, 5

Most Flowering Cherries are trees; several bush types, even though attractive in bloom, are essentially grown for their fruits. Probably the best ornamental shrubby Cherry is the Manchu or Nanking Cherry (*P. tomentosa*), native to northwest China and Japan. Available in bush form is HALLY JOLIVETTE, developed by Dr. Karl Sax of the Arnold Arboretum from *P. subhirtella*. HALLY JOLIVETTE has only recently been commercially available and is highly recommended. It is also available in tree form.

USES    As a specimen; as informal hedge; in mixed shrub borders for background accent; or as a background for a flower garden. Also effective in flower arrangements; branches can be forced for earlier bloom indoors.

HABIT OF GROWTH    Shrubby or like a miniature tree, making a rounded plant up to about 9 feet high.

FLOWERS    Those of *P. tomentosa* are red in bud and open white tinged with pink; ¾ inch across; appear just before the leaves develop, in late April. The fruit that follows is a red Cherry that is edible as well as decorative. The flowers of HALLY JOLIVETTE are semi-double, pale pink, like fluffy balls, and smother the branches over a three-week period.

FOLIAGE    Leaves follow the flowers and are considered attractive.

ASSETS    *Prunus tomentosa* is very hardy (to Zone 3, enduring temperatures to 35 degrees below zero), and in over-all quality is superior to many other flowering fruits that are more commonly grown. HALLY JOLIVETTE, which was developed at the Arnold Arboretum, near Boston, is already rated "choice," which is unusual for a recent novelty. It should be hardy to Zone 5. Flowers of both Flowering Cherries are long lasting.

FAULTS    *Prunus tomentosa* is not listed by many nurseries.

CULTURE    Both forms are easy to grow in full sun, in average, well-drained soil. Prune to shape after flowering.

# FLOWERING CURRANT

TYPE Deciduous
FAMILY *Saxifragaceae* (Sax-iff-rag-*gay*-see-ee)
GENUS *Ribes* (*Rye*-beez)
SPECIES *sanguineum* (san-*gwin*-ee-um)
ZONE 6

The showiest Flowering Currant available today is the variety named KING EDWARD VII. While *Ribes sanguineum* (often called Winter Currant), from which KING EDWARD VII is derived, is native to northern California and the Pacific Northwest, it was introduced in England in the early 1800s and is still better known there than to most American gardeners. (Another Flowering Currant is *Ribes odoratum,* with fragrant yellow flowers, but this is not recommended because it is an alternate host to the White Pine blister rust.)

USES   In the mixed shrub border; at the edge of a woodland or as background accent in a flower garden, where it can be effective with spring-flowering bulbs and early perennials. The English recommend combining it with Forsythia, especially as an informal flowering hedge, with plants of KING EDWARD VII alternating with those of Forsythia.

HABIT OF GROWTH   Upright, sturdy, eventually reaching about 5 to 6 feet.

FLOWERS   Drooping racemes of deep-crimson flowers all along the stems in early spring (April to early May).

FOLIAGE   Downy, soft green leaves, lobed and heart-shaped, developing with the flowers.

ASSETS   Its showy flowers in the spring.

FAULTS   Although considered resistant to the White Pine blister rust, if White Pines are prized and within 900 feet of where the Currant will grow, probably this shrub, along with all other Currants, should be avoided.

CULTURE   Easy in average, well-drained soil. Grow in full sun or light shade. Occasionally thin plants by removing shoots at ground level after flowering. Otherwise prune only to maintain desired shape.

# FLOWERING PLUM

TYPE Deciduous
FAMILY *Rosaceae* (Roz-*ay*-see-ee)
GENUS *Prunus* (*Proon*-us)
SPECIES *triloba* (trye-*loh*-bah)
ZONE 6

This Flowering Plum, sometimes confusingly called Flowering Almond (which see) and "Rose Tree of China" by nursery-catalogue writers, can be pretty as a picture while in full bloom. It is native to China.

USES   Best as an occasional accent in a mixed shrub border or in a flower garden planned for spring flower effect. It can also be trained flat against a wall or fence. Its branches are easily forced into flower when cut in winter and then, as well as at its regular flowering time, are attractive in arrangements.

HABIT OF GROWTH   Compact, miniature tree with a single stem, its ultimate height from 6 to 8 feet.

FLOWERS   Double, bright-pink flowers before the leaves, strung densely along the stems in late April or early May, usually just following Forsythia and at the same time as Bridalwreath Spirea.

FOLIAGE   Broad and rounded, sometimes with three lobes.

ASSETS   The profusion of pretty spring flowers, attractive in the garden with other spring-flowering material.

FAULTS   After flowering, this Plum is a stiff, treelike shrub, not especially attractive in its own right. When combined with other plants of all-season appeal, it can get "lost," which is fine until the next spring, when its showy flowers will again make it prominent in the landscape.

CULTURE   Easy to grow in full sun in well-drained, average soil. Spring planting is to be preferred to fall planting.

PRUNING   Necessary for shaping only; done after flowering. Occasionally remove old stems to encourage new growth, which will flower heavily. When trained as an espalier, annual cutting back of flowering shoots right after blooming will help keep the plant's form and will produce flowering wood for the next season.

# FLOWERING QUINCE

TYPE Deciduous
FAMILY *Rosaceae* (Roz-*ay*-see-ee)
GENUS *Chaenomeles* (Kee-*nom*-el-eez)
SPECIES *japonica* (jap-*pon*-ik-uh), *lagenaria* (lay-jen-*air*-ree-uh)
ZONE 5

The Flowering Quince is a yesteryear's favorite and was prominent in Colonial gardens. (It is one of the featured shrubs in the restored gardens of Colonial Williamsburg.) Some catalogues today list Flowering Quince as *Cydonia*—the botanical name for the Quince grown solely for its fruit. An old-fashioned common name for Flowering Quince is "Japonica."

USES  This very hardy shrub deserves wider planting—especially some of its newer, named forms which are ideal for modern homes and gardens. The low-growing kinds are suitable for foundation and terrace areas; for corner groupings, either massed or combined with other shrubs; and for banks and slopes. The taller varieties are striking in shrub borders, as hedges, and as backgrounds for flower gardens. They are handsome against walls and fences and can be trained as espaliers. They are especially suitable with Tulips and are attractive in arrangements. Branches can be forced into bloom indoors.

HABIT OF GROWTH  Upright yet spreading or mounded in form, with dense, twiggy branches with thorns. Some varieties sucker freely. Ultimate height for most is 6 feet, although there are lower-growing Quinces which reach only 3 feet.

FLOWERS  Single or double, waxy-textured flowers from 1¼ to 2 inches across, profusely produced close to the branches in mid-spring; in some varieties flowers appear before or as the leaves unfold. Colors are brilliant, ranging from fiery reds to coral and orange. There are also pure white varieties. The flowers are followed by edible fruit which can be made into jelly.

FOLIAGE  Alternate, glossy, dark-green leaves, sometimes with a bronze tinge, from 2 to 3 inches long. In mild climates where winter temperatures remain around 30 degrees, the leaves may be semi-evergreen.

ASSETS  The very showy flowers which blaze in the spring landscape, as well as the attractive foliage. A dividend for some might be the fruit, which can be abundant enough to make several jars of jelly.

FAULTS The Flowering Quince can be attacked by San Jose scale and fire blight, although most home gardeners will not be troubled.

CULTURE Average, well-drained soil and full sun. Most Flowering Quinces are super-hardy and will thrive even where winter temperatures go to 20 degrees below zero. (Some varieties, mostly developed on the West Coast, may not be hardy in the colder parts of the North.)

PRUNING Prune after the blossoms have appeared. Good sense must rule the pruning shears. If a specimen Quince in a modified tree form is desired, suckers and low branches can be removed and the whole plant can be thinned. If against a wall and a flat (espalier) form is planned, remove nonconforming growth. In all cases, leggy, less-productive shoots can be shortened.

SPECIES *Chaenomeles japonica.* Dwarf Japanese Quince. Native to Japan. Blood-red flowers, 1½ inches across, in spring at about the same time as Forsythia and often before leafing out. Spreading but low growing (to 3 feet), and useful for this reason.
*C. lagenaria.* Flowering Quince. Native to China. Scarlet flowers, 2 inches across, in early May. Named varieties and hybrids, with average heights about 6 feet unless otherwise indicated, include: CORAL BEAUTY, free flowering, 5 to 6 feet; CRIMSON AND GOLD, velvety dark red with gold stamens; FALCONET CHARLOT, double, salmon-pink, to 7 feet; GLOWING EMBERS, fire-red; KNAPHILL, low growing, to 16–18 inches, orange-scarlet flowers; NIVALIS, outstanding pure white; ROWALLANE, rich red flowers before foliage, low growing, to 30 inches; STANFORD RED, glowing blood-red flowers.

# *FORSYTHIA*

TYPE Deciduous
FAMILY *Oleaceae* (Oh-lee-*ay*-see-ee)
GENUS *Forsythia* (For-*sith*-ee-uh)
SPECIES *intermedia* (in-ter-*meed*-ee-uh), *ovata* (oh-*vay*-tuh),
*suspensa* (sus-*pen*-suh)
ZONE 5

Cheering and cheerful, Forsythia announces that spring has finally arrived. Sometimes called Golden-bells, it is perhaps the most popular spring-flowering shrub in American gardens. The species listed here came from the Orient, although the varieties from them are mostly American originations.

USES Forsythia can be planted singly to make a handsome specimen, or placed in the background of a shrub border for yellow accent in the spring. It makes an informal hedge when each plant can be allowed to grow without shearing. It does not belong in the foundation planting of a house, but specimen plants look well set forward from walls and fences. (Patient gardeners may want to experiment with training a Forsythia as an espalier.) It is ideal on steep banks. Colonies of Forsythias can be established at the edges of woodlands. Early spring-blooming bulbs like Daffodils, Grape-hyacinths, Chionodoxa, and Scillas show well planted near the base of a Forsythia.

HABIT OF GROWTH Forsythia, at its best, forms a graceful, symmetrical shrub with long, arching or upright branches, which, in spring, are clothed in yellow from the tips of the branches to the ground.

FLOWERS This shrub's flowers are always yellow (for the so-called White-forsythia, see Korean Abelia leaf), bell-like in form, and arranged closely on upright or arching branches. There are brilliant as well as pale yellow varieties and the flowers always appear before the foliage in early spring.

FOLIAGE Leaves, which follow the flowers, are opposite and bright green. There are a few variegated varieties which are not especially attractive.

ASSETS It is easy to grow, tolerant of most soils, and pest-free. Its branches can be cut in winter and forced into flower indoors. It is easily propagated by nurseryman and home gardener alike.

FAULTS   Occasionally, after a really severe winter, some, but rarely all, flower buds may be killed by the cold. Japanese beetles like the foliage. Some gardeners ruin its graceful growth by incorrect pruning. Again, because it is so easy to grow and propagate, so reasonable in price, it can be overused, particularly on a small property.

CULTURE   Forsythia likes full sun but will flower in some shade. It will take most soil conditions except excessively dry ones, but will do best in a rich, loamy soil full of organic material (peat moss, leafmold, rotted manure, or compost). Specimen plants will easily fill an area of 10 to 12 feet, although plants can be spaced closer on banks or in informal hedges or colonies. Propagate by cuttings of young wood in early summer.

PRUNING   Correct pruning for forsythia is easy. Every few years, *after flowering,* thin out a few of the oldest branches at the ground level. Never chop Forsythia like a Privet hedge.

SPECIES AND VARIETIES *Forsythia intermedia.* Hybrid between *F. suspensa* and *viridissima.* Its variety *spectabilis,* Showy Border Forsythia, is probably the most common form in gardens. It has bright yellow flowers on erect branches. Choice among newer forms are LYNWOOD GOLD, slightly lighter in color than Showy Border Forsythia, also upright in growth habit, reaching a height of 5 to 7 feet; SPRING GLORY, height 8 feet, a more subtle and paler yellow and perhaps the most appealing Forsythia available today.
*F. ovata.* Recommended for very cold areas where other Forsythias regularly have their flower buds winterkilled. An improvement in this species is BEATRICE FARRAND, with very large, bright yellow flowers on branches reaching 6–8 feet.
*F. suspensa.* Weeping Forsythia. Bright yellow flowers on arching branches which may reach 10 feet. Very commonly grown.

# *FOTHERGILLA*

TYPE Deciduous
FAMILY *Hamamelidaceae* (Ham-am-mel-id-*ay*-see-ee)
GENUS *Fothergilla* (Foth-er-*gill*-uh)
SPECIES *gardeni* (gar-*deen*-eye), *major* (*may*-jor), *monticola*
(mon-*tik*-ol-uh)
ZONE 6

Worth talking about are the odd, fluffy, yet pretty flowers of Fothergilla. All three species are native to parts of the Southeast, but are hardy much farther north.

USES  As specimens, in large shrub borders, in naturalistic plantings or at the edge of woodland. *Fothergilla gardeni* is dwarf enough to be set in a foundation planting. They are especially effective against evergreen backgrounds where their white flowers and bright foliage in fall show especially well.

HABIT OF GROWTH  Erect, yet mounded growth, eventually to about 8 feet in the case of the last two species. *F. gardeni,* Dwarf Fothergilla, grows only about 4 feet high but forms a dense bush as it tends to sucker.

FLOWERS  White flowers with pink stamens in fluffy balls like bottle brushes at the ends of branches in late April or May, as the leaves unfold. They are fragrant.

FOLIAGE  Alternate leaves, about 1 or 2 inches long, deeply veined and resembling those of the Witch-hazel, to which this shrub is related. Their fall color can be striking as they change to yellow, orange and scarlet.

ASSETS  Good native shrubs with attractive spring flowers and pleasing autumn effects in the foliage.

FAULTS  With age, the plants may spread as much as their height, so they need plenty of space. They have been neglected by nurserymen and may be hard to locate.

CULTURE  Grow in well-drained but peaty soil which is able to retain moisture. A slightly acid soil is best and a quantity of peat moss should be added to the planting hole. They can take some shade but autumn foliage color is brightest in full sun or very light shade. Virtually no pruning is necessary other than removing old branches at the ground level if bushes seem crowded, or shortening an unruly branch.

SPECIES *Fothergilla gardeni.* Dwarf Fothergilla. Native from Virginia to Georgia. Rarely exceeds 3 or 4 feet. Flowers generally before the leaves have developed.

*F. major.* Native to Georgia. Upright, to about 8 feet, eventually assuming a pyramidal shape. Flowers appear in mid-May as leaves unfold.

*F. monticola.* Alabama Fothergilla. Native from North Carolina to Alabama. Lower growing than the preceding, it makes a mounded silhouette to about 6 feet and is very effective among Rhododendrons and other evergreens.

# FRANKLIN TREE

TYPE Deciduous
FAMILY *Theaceae* (Tee-*ay*-see-ee)
GENUS *Gordonia* (Gor-*doh*-nee-uh)
SPECIES *alatamaha* (al-at-am-*ay*-huh)
ZONE 6

Of historical interest, this shrub (really a tree in the South but more like a shrub in the North) was first seen in Georgia in 1770 by John Bartram, who took a few plants to his Philadelphia garden. It has not been found in the wild since then, and all plants now being sold are descendants of those original few. This plant is also known as Franklinia.

USES   As a specimen or as background accent in a mixed shrub border.

HABIT OF GROWTH   Many-stemmed, bushy in form; slow growing at first and in the colder parts of the North. Eventually reaches 10 feet or so, up to 30 feet in mild climates.

FLOWERS   Fragrant, cup-shaped flowers, 3 inches across, with white petals and yellow centers. First appearing in late August, they continue through fall until frost. Plants produce some flowers when only 3 or 4 feet high.

FOLIAGE   Handsome, shining leaves, 5 inches long, which turn bright orange-red, striking combined with the flowers.

ASSETS   The showy, fragrant flowers in the fall when few other shrubs are in bloom; the foliage, bright green from spring to late summer, then brilliant orange-red in the fall.

CULTURE   Well-drained but moist soil, full of humus. When planting add peat moss to the soil mixture. The Franklin Tree does best in full sun. While it is hardy to zero and may take 5 to 10 degrees below zero in short doses (plants thrive in protected sections of New England, New York to Ohio, and comparable areas), some winterkill may be expected. Young plants should be protected with leaves or evergreen boughs for the first few winters. No pruning is necessary other than removal of winter-killed portions, if any.

# *FRINGE-TREE*

TYPE Deciduous
FAMILY *Oleaceae* (Oh-lee-*ay*-see-ee)
GENUS *Chionanthus* (Kye-oh-*nanth*-us)
SPECIES *retusa* (re-*tew*-suh), *virginica* (vir-*jin*-ik-cuh)
ZONE 5

Snow-flower is the English meaning of Chionanthus and is as appropriate a common name for this shrub as Fringe-tree or White-fringe. *Chionanthus virginica,* the most common species seen in gardens, is native over a wide region, from Pennsylvania to Florida and west to Missouri and Texas. There is no reason why it can't be grown in more northerly regions in a sheltered position.

USES   The Fringe-tree is usually planted as an accent or specimen on a lawn or as a taller point of interest in a shrub grouping at the corner of a property. Also good placed near a large terrace where it will provide privacy and where its fragrant flowers can be readily enjoyed. In a really wide and extensive shrub border, the Fringe-tree can be used as a background shrub.

HABIT OF GROWTH   In maturity, the Fringe-tree may reach 15 or 25 feet or so, but it is very slow growing. It makes a spreading, treelike pattern with prominent branches.

FLOWERS   They are its glory, literally smothering the plant in late spring (late May to early June in the vicinity of New York) with drooping, loose clusters of pure white, fringed, fragrant petals. The Fringe-tree is dioecious—that is, male and female flowers do not occur on the same plant—and the male flowers are considered somewhat larger and showier. However, it is the female plant that bears handsome, blue Grape-like fruits in the fall. Therefore, the homeowner who has space for two or more of these spreading shrubs should plant a "pair" in order to get the added bonus of fall interest, too.

FOLIAGE   Rather handsome large leaves, glossy, oblong and opposite, which turn yellow in the fall.

ASSETS   One of the better American natives, much prized by the English, and notable for its fragrant flowers and amenable growth—it can be trained by pruning to fit confined areas or allowed to spread when lack of space is not a problem.

FAULTS  It is late to leaf out in the spring compared to other shrubs, but its Ash-like bark and silhouette are not unattractive. It has the same sort of fleshy roots as the Star Magnolia and should be dug carefully so as not to sever their ends. Place it carefully so transplanting won't be necessary.

CULTURE  The Fringe-tree likes full sun and should have a sheltered location in especially cold regions. It needs a well-drained soil, average or somewhat sandy, but needs additional watering in periods of drought.

PRUNING  While the Fringe-tree requires no pruning, it can easily be trained to fit special situations. Low branches can be removed and higher spreading branches can be shortened if a narrower frame is desired. Do this after flowering.

SPECIES  *Chionanthus retusa.* Chinese Fringe-tree. This lesser-known species from China is very similar to *C. virginica* described above but blooms later, usually in July. It should be sought by those who want to keep a continuous display of flowers in their shrub garden.

# GARDENIA

TYPE Evergreen
FAMILY *Rubiaceae* (Roo-bee-*ay*-see-ee)
GENUS *Gardenia* (Gar-*deen*-ee-uh)
SPECIES *jasminoides* (jas-min-*noy*-deez)
ZONE 8

Once the leading corsage flower, the Gardenia has gone out of style for that purpose. It is still a popular landscaping plant in mild climates, and northern gardeners can enjoy it as a house plant if they can provide the necessary coolness. Gardenia, also called Cape-jasmine, is native to China, has been grown and beloved here since Colonial times. There are several named varieties available from nurseries.

USES  In mild climates, as a specimen, especially near an entrance or terrace where its fragrance can be readily appreciated, or among other shrubs, particularly in the foreground of a border. In the North, enjoy it as a pot or tub plant.

HABIT OF GROWTH  Upright, bushy plant which may reach 6 feet but can be restricted to less by pruning or by selecting one of the compact, low-growing kinds available.

FLOWERS  Beautiful waxy, white, sometimes greenish or yellowish flowers, single or double, from spring to fall. The Gardenia flower has one of the most delicious, distinctive perfumes of any flowering shrub.

FOLIAGE  Evergreen, glossy leaves, 4 inches long, and very handsome.

ASSETS  Lovely, fragrant flowers and handsome foliage.

FAULTS  Rather susceptible to several pests, such as mealybug and white fly.

CULTURE  Grow in an acid, rich soil, well-drained but moisture retentive. Add leafmold or peat moss to soil mixture when planting. Grow in full sun or high shade. Fertilize annually with cottonseed meal or commercial fertilizers formulated for Camellias and Azaleas. As a pot plant in the North, the Gardenia must be grown in a cool room (60 to 70 degrees) with high humidity and must receive some sun daily. It benefits from a daily syringing of its foliage. The Gardenia and its flower buds will survive temperatures of about 18 degrees; plants can be wintered over in cold areas when protected by leaves and screening.

PRUNING  On pot plants, pinch back new growth to cause bushiness. In mild climates, prune to shape; occasionally cut back taller shoots partially.

PESTS AND DISEASES  *Chlorosis* of leaves (yellowing of leaves, with veins prominently etched in green) can usually be corrected by applying iron chelates to the soil surface around the plant. *Mealybugs,* white cottony pests, can be controlled by a spray containing malathion. *White fly*—small white flies—can also be controlled by malathion, a poisonous spray to be used with caution.

# GENISTA

TYPE Deciduous
FAMILY *Leguminosae* (Leg-yew-min-*noh*-see)
GENUS *Genista* (Jen-*nist*-uh)
SPECIES *cinerea* (sin-*nee*-ree-uh), *germanica* (jer-*man*-ik-uh), *hispanica* (hiss-*pan*-ik-uh), *pilosa* (pye-*loh*-suh), *sagittalis* (saj-it-*tay*-lis), *tinctoria* (tink-*tor*-ee-uh)
ZONE See descriptions of species, below

Genista is another Broom (Cytisus), the two genera being so similar that only a botanist can tell the various species apart. (According to botanists, the seeds of Genista lack an appendage, or "wart," at the base of the seed.) The Genista that florists offer in pots around Easter time is not a Genista: it is *Cytisus canariensis*. The Genista or Sweet Broom grown on the West Coast is also a Cytisus—*Cytisus racemosa*. There are some tall-growing species of Genista seen in Europe which are not generally available in this country. The species listed here are true members of the genus, most suited to rock gardens and ground-cover use. They are native to Europe.

USES  As ground covers in sunny, dry areas and in the rock garden.

HABIT OF GROWTH  Generally mounds, low-growing and trailing; the stems and shoots are bright green, occasionally thorny. Height of these species rarely exceeds 3 feet.

FLOWERS  Pealike, bright-yellow flowers in racemes or clusters, in late May or June.

FOLIAGE  Sparse, alternate leaves, sometimes trifoliate.

ASSETS  The mass of bright yellow flowers, like a basket of gold. Also the plant's tolerance of sunny, dry situations. Excellent nestled among low rocks.

FAULTS  Difficult to transplant; need special conditions.

CULTURE  Grow in sunny, well-drained sandy soil to which peat moss is added in planting hole. Plant in spring from pots— the way most nurseries offer plants. Don't disturb once plant is settled. In cold areas, provide airy winter cover of evergreen boughs. Prune only as necessary to shape.

SPECIES *Genista cinerea*. Native to southern Europe. Hardy in Zone 7 or where temperatures remain above 5 degrees. Height about 3 feet. Yellow flowers in racemes about 8 inches long, in early June. Suitable for slopes, banks, sunny areas.

*G. germanica.* Low, spiny branches with bright yellow flowers in late May and early June. Native to Europe. Hardy to zero. Height about 2 feet. For ground cover and rock gardens in full sun.

*G. hispanica.* Spanish Gorse. Spiny green stems and twigs, with bright yellow flowers in early June. Native to Europe. Height about 2 feet. Choice in dry, sunny locations. Hardy to about 5 degrees.

*G. pilosa.* European native, very low growing (not above 1 foot), and fine ground cover for lean, dry soil. It will tolerate light shade, as under high trees. Hardy to Zone 6. Bright yellow flowers in spring show well against mound of silvery-green foliage.

*G. sagittalis.* Native to southern Europe. Short racemes of yellow flowers in late May to June. Height about 1 foot or less, making it a true ground cover for sunny, dry soils. Very hardy (to Zone 5—10 to 20 degrees below zero).

*G. tinctoria.* Native to Europe and western Asia. Yellow flowers in early June which show well against green twigs and stems. Height about 3 feet. Very hardy. Zone 2.

# GLOSSY ABELIA

TYPE Semi-evergreen
FAMILY *Caprifoliaceae* (Kap-rif-foh-lee-*ay*-see-ee)
GENUS *Abelia* (Ab-*beel*-ee-uh)
SPECIES *grandiflora* (gran-dif-*floh*-ruh)
ZONE 5

Pleasing yet never flamboyant, the Glossy Abelia is a hybrid between two species, *Abelia chinensis* and *A. uniflora,* both natives of China. It is by far the most popular Abelia now available in American nurseries and is especially popular in the South. Glossy Abelia is classed as semi-evergreen because, while its leaves are reliably evergreen and its stems are rarely injured by cold from Philadelphia southward, in New England and comparable climates it often behaves as a die-back shrub, with new growth appearing each spring. The Glossy Abelia is one parent of still another hybrid, Abelia EDWARD GOUCHER, also popular in the South and on the West Coast.

USES  First as a part of any mixed shrub planting, usually toward the front where it makes a graceful accent or blender—depending on its neighbors. Secondary uses are in foundation plantings, where it goes well with other broad-leaved evergreens; as an informal, untrimmed hedge or screen; and occasionally as a specimen accent plant. Abelia EDWARD GOUCHER can be used in similar fashion to the Glossy Abelia. A recently introduced variety of the Glossy Abelia called PROSTRATA is recommended as a ground cover. It has white flowers.

HABIT OF GROWTH  It makes a loose, graceful bush, its slender branches slightly arching, varying in length from 4 feet in cold climates to 6 or 8 feet in more moderate areas.

FLOWERS  Mildly fragrant, pink funnel-shaped flowers about ¾ inch long, in clusters at the ends of branches or at the leaf axils. The flowers are similar to those of some Honeysuckles. Abelia is, in fact, a member of the Honeysuckle family. The flowers appear first in early summer and continue into the late fall.

FOLIAGE  Dark, glossy green leaves which become bronze in late summer. They are opposite and about 1½ inches long.

ASSETS  Glossy Abelia, after late spring, is in continual flower until stopped by cold weather—reason enough for having it around. Its foliage, cool, shining and bronzy, is attractive throughout the spring, summer and fall in cold climates and year round in moderate and warm areas where winter injury is not a probability. Sprays of Glossy Abelia are attractive in flower arrangements. It is free from pests and diseases.

FAULTS  During some winters in areas where Glossy Abelia's evergreen character is uncertain, the foliage may become burned and scarred from winter injury and yet be persistent, making it unattractive.

CULTURE  An easy-to-grow shrub, needing only well-drained soil to which some peat moss or other humus has been added at time of planting. It will take full sun or light shade but should not be placed in excessively windy locations. On Long Island and southward and on the West Coast this shrub can make a spread of 6 feet or so and an allowance should be made for this at the time of planting. At any rate, don't crowd Abelia or its charm will be lost. This is an easy-to-propagate shrub for home gardeners who can take cuttings in early July, insert them in a mixture of sand and peat moss in a flat or pot, and after soaking thoroughly, cover with plastic film. In about five weeks, the cuttings will be rooted and can then be set out in a protected spot in open ground.

PRUNING  In early spring, cut back any stems that are straggly or winter injured. Don't chop—let the shrub always assume its naturally graceful and arching habit.

# HARDY-ORANGE

TYPE  Deciduous
FAMILY  *Rutaceae*  (Rew-*tay*-see-ee)
GENUS  *Poncirus*  (Pon-*sye*-rus)
SPECIES  *trifoliata*  (trye-foh-lee-*ay*-tuh)
ZONE  6

The idea of growing Citrus in cold climates is intriguing to many gardeners. This close relative of the true Orange is hardy to 10 degrees below zero. It comes from northern China and Korea and has been grown in this country since the mid-1800s. Apart from its ornamental interest, it has been of value as a understock for Oranges, thereby extending their hardiness range. The "Citrange" is a hybrid fruit obtained by crossing the Hardy-orange with the Sweet Orange.

USES   In the upper South, the Hardy Orange makes a rugged hedge; farther north it is usually grown as a specimen, best somewhat protected as against a wall or fence where its odd, evergreen frame shows well. Its stiff yet interesting form is especially suited to very modern architecture. It can also be grown in tubs.

HABIT OF GROWTH   Upright, stiff, its angular branches protected by stout thorns or spines, to 8 or 10 feet or more in the South, but less in cold climates. The bright green of its branches and spines is attractive, especially in winter.

FLOWERS   White flowers, 2 inches across, fragrant, in the axils of the spines in late April or May, before the leaves unfurl. The yellow-orange fruits that follow are miniature "oranges," rather wizened and downy yet aromatic and showy. They are not considered edible, being very dry, acid and bitter, yet the thrifty English make conserve from them.

FOLIAGE   The three to five leaflets, leathery and sparsely produced, are carried on typical Citrus winged petioles.

ASSETS   This shrub is a curiosity, even a "conversation piece" in the North, yet in the right setting it possesses charm. Certainly its flowers and fruit, which show up well against the bright green, spiny branches, are attractive.

FAULTS   Too exotic in appearance for most garden settings.

CULTURE  The Hardy-orange grows in full sun in well-drained, moderately rich soil full of humus. When planting, add leafmold or peat moss to the planting hole.

PRUNING  Essential in the North only for training, best after the flowers have bloomed. When the Hardy-orange is planted as a hedge, it responds well to shearing, forming a more impenetrable barrier.

# *HARLEQUIN GLORY-BOWER*

TYPE Deciduous
FAMILY *Verbenaceae* (Ver-ben-*nay*-see-ee)
GENUS *Clerodendron* (Kleer-oh-*den*-dron)
SPECIES *trichotomum* (trye-*kot*-om-um)
ZONE 6

Despite the glamorous connotation evoked by this shrub's name, it is more a plant for large estates or botanic gardens than for today's space-limited home gardens. What is more, it is rarely listed by nurseries. It is native to Japan.

USES  Difficult because of its suckering habit and exotic appearance. However, it can be trained to a single stem, and grown this way, or as a colony, it would make an interesting accent in a modern setting—with pebbles, stones, and the like as accompanying accessories.

HABIT OF GROWTH  Tall, with many suckers, to 7–10 feet.

FLOWERS  Fragrant, white flowers in small clusters from the upper leaf axils, in August. Showy bright-blue berries, surrounded by a red calyx, follow to make an effective fall display.

FOLIAGE  Large, coarse leaves, 5 inches long, which are gray and hairy.

ASSETS  The fragrant, attractive flowers and showy fruits.

FAULTS  Too exotic and spreading for the average home garden.

CULTURE  Easy to grow in full sun and moderately rich soil. Suckers can be cut off, but new ones will appear. In the North, some winterkill may occur; in this case, the stems can be cut back to the ground or to live buds.

# HEATH

TYPE Evergreen
FAMILY *Ericaceae* (Ehr-ik-*ay*-see-ee)
GENUS *Erica* (*Ehr*-ik-uh)
SPECIES *carnea* (*kar*-nee-uh), *ciliaris* (sil-ee-*ay*-riss), *cinerea* (sin-*neer*-ee-uh), *hybrida* (hy-*brid*-uh), *mediterranea* (med-it-er-*ray*-nee-uh), *tetralix* (tet-*ray*-licks), *vagans* (*vay*-ganz)
ZONE See descriptions of species, below

This is the true Heath (see Heather, its close relative). There are winter-blooming as well as summer-blooming Heaths and, fortunately for gardeners in areas where the soil is not acid, many Heaths will thrive in slightly alkaline or neutral soil. There are Erica species native to the British Isles, Europe, and South Africa.

USES  Heaths are suitable for rock gardens, for covering slopes and steep banks, for using as edgings or as informal hedges, for massing in flower gardens and in front of taller-growing shrubs such as Azaleas and Rhododendrons, and on top of or at the base of retaining walls. A few Heaths can stand alone as handsome accent plants, while others fit into such contemporary adjuncts as planter boxes and terrace edgings. Best of all, Heaths vary so much among themselves that they can make their own garden. Some of the tender Heaths are important cut-flower crops on the West Coast for the florist market.

HABIT OF GROWTH  Erica species and varieties range from creeping, almost ground-hugging, plants to mounded or bushy shrubs from 1½ to 4 feet high.

FLOWERS  The long-lasting flowers (technically, each is a corolla) are urn-shaped or bell-shaped, often with prominent stamens; they hang from short racemes, and are bright-colored and profuse enough to make very showy effects. Their colors range from white to rose, red, and purple. There are Heaths that flower in winter, spring, summer, and fall.

FOLIAGE  Evergreen, needlelike leaves which are opposite and in whorls around the stem, somewhat reminiscent of those of Spruce and other cone-bearing evergreens. As with the Heathers, the foliage color varies greatly, from dark and light greens to yellow and bronze and gray. The bronze tints are especially intense during winter.

ASSETS  Heaths offer interest all the year, and are ideal plants for the collector and rock-garden enthusiast. They also appeal to the modern gardener who seeks tough shrubs of year-round value with low maintenance requirements. They are of special value to the seashore gardener.

FAULTS They are not suited to heavy clay soils, and not all will thrive in non-acid soils. In New England and other northern regions, some winter burning of the foliage may occur.

CULTURE Heaths require well-drained, sandy soil which contains humus in the form of peat (peat moss and/or leafmold), and which is acid. Yet it has been discovered that they will do well in a fair variety of soils with the exception of very heavy, poorly drained ones. An average loam or a gravelly or stony soil that may be too lean for the diets of other shrubs can be very satisfactory. Some Heaths are tolerant of neutral or slightly alkaline soils. These include *Erica carnea,* an especially hardy, rugged species which makes an excellent ground cover and which is the most readily available Heath from American nurseries; and *Erica mediterranea.* When planting, set the plants deeply or at least so that their needlelike foliage is resting on the soil. This forces new roots to form, thus enabling the plants to become quickly established and to make strong new growth. Plants that have been set too high often languish and may even die. If there is any doubt concerning the planting level of plants, it is best to dig them and replant in a deeper hole. Although peat moss and/or leafmold are the best humus-forming materials to incorporate in planting holes, rotted sawdust, compost, thoroughly rotted manure, or Michigan peat make good substitutes. Pine needles and wood chips are good materials to use as mulch around Heaths and their relatives. Heaths are essentially sun lovers, but again *Erica carnea* does very well beneath tall trees such as Oaks and Pines. Once established, Heaths are drought resistant, require no feeding. Ericas are usually shipped by mail-order nurseries in early spring or fall, but plants from local nurseries can be lifted and replanted at almost any time when the soil is workable. All plants must be well watered immediately after being set out.

PRUNING   Shear off winter-burned foliage in the spring and remove faded flower racemes to keep growth compact. In general, though, light pruning is all that is required and where plants are thriving and not straggly, none is essential.

PROPAGATION   The collector or Heath hobbyist is bound to become interested in increasing these plants. The four methods are by seeds, cuttings, layering, and division. By far the easiest method for the home gardener is by layering, especially as the plants will do this naturally if their side branches are in constant contact with a humusy mulch. The gardener can expedite the process by pegging down side branches with a hairpin, bent wire, or stone. After it has rooted the branch is then severed from its parent plant, dug carefully so as not to unduly disturb its hairlike roots, and replanted at once in a new site.

SPECIES AND VARIETIES   *Erica carnea.* Spring Heath, Alpine Forest Heath. Native to Europe. Mat-forming dwarf, to about 6 inches, with light-green foliage and rose flowers in late winter, early spring; blooms are made more prominent by their exserted stamens. Tolerant of drought, poor soil, and lime, this is the most accommodating of all Ericas. It is hardy to Zone 6 and, if protected, in even colder areas. It has many varieties.
*E. ciliaris.* Dorset Heath. From western Europe. Trailing habit, to 9–12 inches high. Rosy-purple flowers in late summer. Associates well with Azaleas. Zone 6.
*E. cinerea.* Bell Heath, Scotch or Gray Heath, Twisted Heath. Native to British Isles. Height 2 feet. It has escaped from gardens in New England and has become naturalized. Egg-shaped flowers from white to purple, in dense upright clusters in summer. Hardy to Zone 6. Variety C. D. EASON has deep-green foliage and bright rose-pink bells which may appear from early summer into fall.
*E. hybrida.* The Heaths of hybrid origin are many, especially in England, yet several are available in the United States. These include DARLYENSIS (*E. mediterranea* and *E. carnea*), about 8 inches tall, with early-blooming, rose flowers. Hardy to Zone 6.
*E. mediterranea.* Mediterranean Heath. Hardiest of the tall-growing treelike Heaths from western Europe. It has fragrant red

flowers in spring, attractive against dark-green, dense foliage. Height 3–4 feet. There are white and lavender varieties as well as hybrids available from specialists. Hardy in protected areas of Zone 7.

*E. tetralix.* Cross-leaved Heath. Native to moors of Europe. Rosy flowers and gray foliage on 10-inch plants. Many varieties, including GEORGE FRASER, gray-leaved with large rose flowers from June to October; MOLLIS, dark-gray foliage with white flowers in summer. Zone 6.

*E. vagans.* Cornish Heath. Native to Europe and British Isles, where it makes a rounded shrub 3 feet high but with a spread of 4 to 5 feet. It has glossy green leaves and pale-lilac flowers from late summer to autumn. There are many varieties. Hardy to Zone 7.

# *HEATHER*

TYPE Evergreen
FAMILY *Ericaceae* (Ehr-ik-*ay*-see-ee)
GENUS *Calluna* (Kal-*lew*-nuh)
SPECIES *vulgaris* (vul-*gay*-riss)
ZONE 5

This is the Scotch Heather or Ling which covers the moors of Great Britain. It is also the plant cultivated in vast quantities on the West Coast to supply florists with long-lasting spikes of rose-colored flowers during the winter and spring months. In various parts of New England and Nova Scotia, Heather plants have become so extensively naturalized as to appear to be native. Still, this is a shrub whose fine qualities and general usefulness Americans are just beginning to appreciate.

USES  Although Calluna possesses but one species, there are many varieties, varying considerably in height. There are varieties that can be placed in front of larger shrubs such as Azaleas and Rhododendrons, used in foundation plantings, on banks and slopes as ground cover, along walks or drives as a sort of hedge. There are Heather varieties that are effective on the top of retaining walls or in rock gardens. It is a most desirable shrub for gardeners near seashore areas. The flower spikes are valuable for flower arrangers and are easily dried, retaining their colors faithfully.

HABIT OF GROWTH  Upright, rather stiff but interesting form up to 3 feet, but there are varieties like FOXI which make intriguing pincushions only 4 inches high. Other varieties fall between these two height extremes, the average perhaps being around 18 inches.

FLOWERS  Heather flowers over a long period, the first varieties starting in early summer, others continuing in summer and fall. All flower spikes are long lasting. The individual flowers, which may be single or double, are about ⅛ inch long but are crowded on the stems so profusely that their floral effect is definitely showy. The single flowers are bell-shaped; the double flowers look like exquisitely executed needlework. Colors are typically rosy-purple, but there are white as well as red, deep rose, light pink, and purple varieties.

FOLIAGE  Tiny, scalelike leaves, opposite, and arranged on the stems in whorls to give a four-dimensional effect. They are evergreen and vary from bright green to yellow, golden, pinkish and silvery and gray. In winter the foliage of some varieties turns to interesting gold, copper, and bronze.

ASSETS   Heather abounds in versatility, both as to its varieties and its place in the landscape. The refinement of its flowers and foliage, its low maintenance requirements and its all-season value make it a truly distinctive shrub. For the collector, the study and establishment of a Heather garden (along with its close Heath relatives) and the study of its history, distribution and many varieties makes a fascinating hobby.

FAULTS   The only point that can be mentioned here is that the Heather's soil requirements must be met (see below).

CULTURE   First of all, the Heather, being a member of the Heath family (*Ericaceae*), needs an acid, well-drained soil, probably the ideal being a sandy loam to which large amounts of leafmold and/or peat moss have been added. Other forms of humus can be used—rotted sawdust or lime-free homemade compost, to name two. The Heather has a far-reaching, fine root system and stiff clay soil is not to its liking. Heathers are essentially sun-lovers but will tolerate light shade for a part of a day and still bloom satisfactorily. Plants can be set or moved successfully during the growing season, but should be well watered to keep the fine roots from drying out. Plants are usually bought with a ball of earth around their roots. Today many growers ship young plants in peat pots, in which case the pot may be planted too. When ordering Heathers, always plant three or more of a kind. Set the plants at least as deep as they were formerly growing, and on banks or slopes, it is well to break the general rule and set the plants even deeper, up to the start of the foliage, say. Spacing of Heather plants depends on how they are being used and the age of the plant that has been purchased. Young plants of the taller growing varieties (AUREA, MRS. H. E. BEALE, etc.), although upright in habit, will make a spread of 16 inches or so and therefore need spacing of about the same distance to accommodate this eventual spread. Mulching the soil surface around Heathers is a good practice: use well-rotted leafmold, compost, sawdust. Some peat moss can be mixed with the preceding, but peat moss as a mulch alone, unless it can be lightly and carefully incorporated with the soil, should be avoided. Pine needles make an excellent permanent mulching for Heathers.

PROPAGATION Heathers can be easily increased by layering, that is, by pegging a long shoot to the soil by means of a hairpin. Rooted layers can be severed from the parent in spring. A second method is to take cuttings in early summer, insert them in a mixture of moist sand and peat moss in a flat or box, and cover with polyethylene. They should root in about four weeks.

PRUNING Leggy plants or those with branch tips that have been burned during the winter as well as spent flower stalks can all be trimmed in the spring. The resulting new growth will be vigorous and floriferous. Varieties of Heather that bloom in early summer can have flower racemes removed as they fade.

PESTS AND DISEASES No troubles of any seriousness, but occasionally a Heather plant starts to brown at the center, the trouble progressing upward, leaving naked center and stems. A suggested remedy is to lift the plant and reset it much deeper in the soil, so deep that all the brown part is underground. Such treatment may cause the plants to form new roots as well as arrest the original difficulty.

VARIETIES One English specialist nursery lists over 40 varieties of Heather, *Calluna vulgaris*. In the United States and Canada, far fewer varieties are available but all are top notch. Some good ones are:
AUREA, 18 inches high, leaves bright yellow, turning red-bronze in winter, lilac flowers in July to September; ELSIE FRYE, 18 inches, double white flowers in July to September; COUNTY WICKLOW, 12–15 inches, double pink flowers in late summer; MRS. J. H. HAMILTON, prostrate growth to 10 inches, bright double pink flowers from midsummer on; FOXI, mound growth, to 4 inches; MRS. H. E. BEALE, 24 inches, double pink flowers in early summer; MRS. PAT, 12 inches, lavender flowers, tips of new foliage pinkish; MRS. R. H. GRAY, prostrate growth to 4 inches, lavender flowers in midsummer.

# *HOLLY-OLIVE*

TYPE Evergreen
FAMILY *Oleaceae* (Oh-lee-*ay*-see-ee)
GENUS *Osmanthus* (Os-*manth*-us)
SPECIES *Delavayi* (De-lay-*vay*-eye), *Fortunei* (For-*toon*-eye), *il-icifolius* (il-iss-if-*foh*-lee-us)
ZONE See descriptions of species, below

Hollylike except for its more prominent, very fragrant flowers. In fact the name Osmanthus means "scent flower." The species described here are from Japan.

USES  As a specimen for accent; as clipped hedge; against a wall; as an espalier. The cut foliage is as effective as Holly in arrangements.

HABIT OF GROWTH  Upright and shapely, like the English Holly. In the North, Osmanthus grows slowly, remains compact.

FLOWERS  Clusters of small white or greenish-white tubular flowers, Jasminelike, in spring or early summer. They are delightfully fragrant. The fruit that follows is dark blue.

FOLIAGE  Beautiful evergreen leaves, like those of English Holly, even to the spines, except for the fact that the leaves of Holly-olive are opposite. There are several variegated forms.

ASSETS  Handsome foliage plants, with the dividend of scented flowers.

FAULTS  Lack of hardiness for most northern regions.

CULTURE  Grow in sun or light shade in well-drained, humusy soil. Shelter from wind, especially in the North, is essential.

PRUNING  None is needed except for training or for shearing, if Osmanthus is grown as a formal hedge.

SPECIES AND VARIETIES  *Osmanthus Delavayi.* Delavay Osmanthus. Native to China. (Botanically it is called *Siphonosmanthus Delavayi,* but in the trade is still listed as *Osmanthus.*) Hardy in Zone 7, it will take winter temperatures down to 5 or 10 degrees. Its flowers are very fragrant, its branches arching. Very useful for the West Coast and other mild-climate areas.
*O. Fortunei.* Hybrid of *O. ilicifolius* and the old conservatory and greenhouse favorite, *O. fragrans.* It, too, has charming fragrant flowers, good habit and Hollylike leaves. Height about 6 feet.

Hardy in Zone 8; stands about 10 degrees as lowest winter temperature. Another choice plant for the South and the West Coast. *O. ilicifolius.* Formerly *O. aquifolius.* Hardy to Zone 7 (0 to 10 degrees), this shrub can be grown in the North if protected from winter winds. Ideal against warm walls or in bays where it remains an attractive accent, growing slowly. In the South and on the West Coast, it makes a formal hedge. Eventual height, 10 feet or more. There are variegated forms.

# HONEYSUCKLE

TYPE Deciduous and evergreen
FAMILY *Caprifoliaceae* (Kap-rif-foh-lee-*ay*-see-ee)
GENUS *Lonicera* (Lon-*niss*-er-uh)
SPECIES *amoena* (am-*meen*-uh), *bella* (*bell*-uh), *fragrantissima*
(fray-gran-*tiss*-im-uh), *Korolkowi* (Koh-rol-*koh*-wye), *Maacki*
(*Mack*-eye), *Morrowi* (*Mor*-row-eye), *tatarica* (tat-*tar*-ik-uh)
ZONE See descriptions of species, below

Not all Honeysuckles are vines. These shrubby, upright forms are hardy and versatile in their value as well as attractive. Some are hybrids, their parents coming from Asia.

USES  As informal hedges and screens; as background for flower gardens; as occasional accents in the rear of large, mixed shrub planting; as specimens; and in semi-naturalistic settings, where they will endure high shade. Winter Honeysuckle (*L. fragrantissima*) has fragrant flowers, easily forced into early bloom indoors. All have berries that are especially attractive to birds.

HABIT OF GROWTH  Generally large and tall, spreading plants, rounded or moundlike, with gracefully arching branches.

FLOWERS  Bell-shaped or tubular flowers, often with two lips, in pairs all along the branches. Blooming time is from April (Winter Honeysuckle) through May and early June. Fruit is effective and appears in summer, lasting as long as the birds let it. Not all flowers of bush forms of the Honeysuckle are fragrant.

FOLIAGE  Deciduous or semi-evergreen leaves, opposite, sometimes blue-green in color.

ASSETS  The abundance of pretty flowers, sometimes fragrant; the attractive habit of the shrub; and showy berries, liked by birds. They are hardy and easy to grow.

FAULTS  Honeysuckles are large shrubs—both in height and spread—and may outgrow original positions or may require restraining by annual pruning.

CULTURE  Grow in well-drained, average soil. Honeysuckles are easy to establish and to transplant.

PRUNING  When space is no problem, allow these shrubs to assume their own spreading form. Occasionally remove old stems at the base to force growth of young vigorous wood. Don't chop or hack—if this seems necessary to keep them down to size, the plants are probably misplaced.

SPECIES AND HYBRIDS  *Lonicera amoena.* Hybrid between *L. tatarica* and *L. Korolkowi.* Graceful, arching bush to about 9 feet. Many flowers, pink or white, in mid-spring. Variety ARNOLDIANA has white flowers, flushed with pink; variety ROSEA has pink flowers. Red berries appear in midsummer. Zone 6.

*L. bella.* Hybrids of *L. tatarica* and *L. Morrowi,* with pink to white flowers in late May. Choice for both flowers and fruit. Zone 5.

*L. fragrantissima.* Winter Honeysuckle. Early flowers (mid-April), white and very fragrant, and leathery leaves that are evergreen in the South and partially so in the North. It reaches 6 feet. Flowers are produced on the previous year's wood. Cut branches force easily. Zone 6 (to zero).

*L. Korolkowi.* Blue-leaf Honeysuckle. Rose-colored flowers in late May. This shrub, which may reach 12 feet, is especially distinctive because of its blue foliage. Very common in nurseries now is the variety ZABELLI, with flowers of a strong red-purple, very showy. Zone 5.

*L. Maacki.* Amur Honeysuckle. Fragrant white flowers that turn to yellow, in late May, followed by dark red berries. Tall-growing, it may reach 15 feet or more. Suitable for a strong hedge or screen. Zone 3.

*L. Morrowi.* White flowers, turning to yellow, in late May. Grows 6 feet high, forming a rounded, dense bush. It has dark red berries. Variety XANTHOCARPA has yellow fruits. Zone 4 (to 20 degrees below zero).

*L. tatarica.* Tatarian Honeysuckle. Flowers pink, red, and white. There are many varieties, including ARNOLD RED, with very dark red flowers, considered choice. CLAVEY'S DWARF has fragrant white flowers. Plant is neat, compact, to 4 feet. Zone 3.

# *HYDRANGEA*

TYPE Deciduous
FAMILY *Saxifragaceae* (Sax-iff-rag-*gay*-see-ee)
GENUS *Hydrangea* (Hye-*drayn*-jee-uh)
SPECIES *arborescens* (ar-bor-*ress*-senz), *grandiflora* (gran-dif-*floh*-ruh), *macrophylla* (mak-roh-*fill*-uh), *paniculata* (pan-ik-yew-*lay*-tuh), *quercifolia* (kwer-sif-*foh*-lee-uh)
ZONE See descriptions of species, below

This popular summer-flowering shrub is so universal that it is readily recognized by gardener and non-gardener alike. Surprisingly, several Hydrangea species are native to this country; the so-called "French" or florist's Hydrangea comes from Japan.

USES Unfortunately, Hydrangeas often just get planted, no prior thought having been given to their use. *H. arborescens* and its variety *grandiflora,* called Hills-of-Snow, is often used as a low hedge along a drive or walk. A better use for today is placing three or four plants in the foreground of a shrub border or grouping so that their billowy, snowy flowers are viewed from some distance and are set off by a lawn and other shrubs. In special cases, plants can be used around terraces or as a low hedge for the foundation planting. The PeeGee Hydrangea (*H. paniculata grandiflora*) can be used in the background of mixed shrub borders and plantings, its 12-inch flower pyramids making an interesting accent in late summer. It makes a tall, informal flowering hedge. It can be trained as a tree and used as a lawn accent, but there are far more refined plants available for this purpose. The PeeGee's flowers may be cut in the pink stage and dried for arrangements. The French Hydrangea (*H. Macrophylla*) and its many forms fit into shrub borders or as background and accent in a flower garden. It also makes a good tub plant for terraces. The Oakleaf Hydrangea (*H. quercifolia*) is distinctive enough for specimen use toward the outskirts of a lawn, under high trees, or in naturalistic settings.

HABIT OF GROWTH Bushy, upright plants, sometimes tree-like if trained to a single stem. The illustration shows the habit of a French Hydrangea.

FLOWERS Panicles or rounded or platelike heads of flowers, in some cases the outer flowers being sterile, in white, pink, or blue, in early summer to fall, depending on species. Illustrated here are close-ups of the PeeGee, French and Oakleaf Hydrangea flowers.

FOLIAGE Large, often coarse leaves, opposite and lobed.

ASSETS   Valuable for showy summer flowers. Some varieties of the French Hydrangea produce dainty, lacy flower patterns quite distinct from the huge panicles of other kinds. Pink and blue colors of the French type are so bright as to appear "painted." Most are hardy; all are easy to grow and make rapid growth.

FAULTS   Overexposure! A few years ago, everyone planted the Hydrangea. Except for the Oakleaf Hydrangea, the plants offer little except their flowers.

CULTURE   Easy to grow in full sun in well-drained but moisture-retentive soil. The French Hydrangeas, especially, need ample watering in drought periods. When planting, add quantities of organic material to the soil. Aluminum sulphate, about 1 lb. per square yard of surface, will make pink-flowered French Hydrangeas turn blue if they are growing in non-acid soil. In acid soil, the flowers naturally remain blue. Adding lime to acid soil will change blue flowers to pink. Only the flower color of French Hydrangea can be changed.

PRUNING   Pruning depends on whether flower buds are formed on wood of the previous season or on new growth. See recommendations under descriptions of the species that follow.

SPECIES AND VARIETIES   *Hydrangea arborescens.* Native from New York to Florida and Louisiana. White flowers. Height about 10 feet. Its form *grandiflora,* Hills-of-Snow, is much more common. Cream-white flowers in early summer. Blooms on new growth, so if tops are winterkilled or plants cut back in early spring, resulting new shoots will produce flowers. Height about 3 to 4 feet. Very hardy (Zone 4).

*H. macrophylla.* French or House Hydrangea. From Japan. These are the bright pink, white, or blue Hydrangeas sold in pots by florists in the spring. There are many varieties, some with rounded flower heads, others with flat, lacelike heads due to combination of perfect flowers in the center surrounded by sterile flowers. These varieties are reasonably hardy where temperatures remain above zero, and for this reason are widely grown outdoors in the South and on the West Coast. However, they are also satisfactory on Cape Cod, Long Island, and in southern New York and to the vicinity of Philadelphia, only occasionally suffering winter damage. Flowers of this species come from terminal buds produced in the previous year, so in cold areas these buds are often injured, with the result that the plant makes leaf growth but produces no flowers. Gardeners in cold regions sometimes surround the plants with a screen or wire frame filled with leaves to protect the flower buds. Spring pruning prevents flowering; prune after the plants have bloomed. A few varieties of this species offered by nurseries for growing outdoors include MARIESI, PARSIVAL, NIKKO BLUE. In acid soil, flowers tend to be very bright blue; in alkaline soil, bright pink; and pale blue in near-neutral soils.

*H. paniculata grandiflora.* PeeGee Hydrangea. From Japan. Large, long panicles of white, sterile flowers which fade to pink. It is very common in midsummer gardens. Height depends on training and use; "tree" forms may reach 20 feet or more, but usual height is about 8 to 10 feet. Flowers are produced on new spring growth, so early spring pruning should be practiced to remove thin, weak shoots. Leave only strong stems, with two buds each, to avoid the floppy effect given by stems that are too light to support the heavy flowers. Very hardy. Zone 4.

*H. quercifolia.* Oakleaf Hydrangea. Native from Georgia to Florida and Mississippi. Next to some of the "lace" forms of the French Hydrangea, this native is considered more desirable than the common Hydrangeas. Loose panicles of white flowers which fade to pink and rose, and distinctive large Oaklike leaves which turn to red and purplish tints in the fall. Height about 5 feet; spreads by stolons. It is best as an accent, under tall trees or at the edge of woodland, or in naturalistic plantings. It takes light shade. Hardy in Zone 5 where temperatures don't go below 10 degrees below zero. Needs little pruning.

# IRISH-HEATH

TYPE Evergreen
FAMILY *Ericaceae* (Ehr-ik-*ay*-see-ee)
GENUS *Daboecia* (Dab-oh-*eesh*-ee-uh)
SPECIES *cantabrica* (kan-*tab*-rik-uh)
ZONE 6, 7

Yes, Ireland has its Heath, too, although it must share this small evergreen with Spain, where it is also a native. Found in parts of southwestern Ireland, Irish-heath is known as St. Dabeoc's Heath and as Connemara Heath.

USES  Any acid soil situation as a ground cover, as a low-growing companion to Azaleas and Rhododendrons and other members of the Heath family, as well as in special problem areas involving banks and slopes. Also on top of dry walls and in rock gardens.

HABIT OF GROWTH  Small and upright, to 2 feet or under.

FLOWERS  Papery textured, egg-shaped "bells," about ½ inch long, in clusters at the ends of branches, varying in color from white to rose to a combination of both. Irish-heath is virtually everblooming, some flowers appearing from spring to fall.

FOLIAGE  The evergreen leaves are a lustrous dark green above, very white underneath; they crowd the stems in an alternate arrangement.

ASSETS  Its everblooming habit and value in the Heath garden.

FAULTS  It must be grown in an acid soil, a limiting factor for gardeners in many parts of the United States. Plants may suffer winter injury in exposed situations unless mulched.

CULTURE  Grow in an acid, sandy soil, full of peat moss. It needs more moisture than do *Erica* and *Calluna*. It can be planted in partial shade and seems to flower there as well as when growing in completely open situations.

PRUNING  It requires a yearly removal of the old flower spikes in winter or early spring and removal of winterkilled tops in early spring.

SPECIES AND VARIETIES *Daboecia cantabrica* has magenta-colored, bell-like flowers in racemes varying from a few inches long to 6 or 7. A variety, ALBA, has larger flowers, white, especially attractive on spikes which may reach 12 inches in length.

# JAPANESE SNOWBELL

TYPE Deciduous
FAMILY *Styracaceae* (Stye-rah-*kay*-see-ee)
GENUS *Styrax* (*Stye*-rax)
SPECIES *japonica* (jap-*pon*-ik-uh)
ZONE 6

Whether classed as a large shrub or a small tree, the Japanese Snowbell (sometimes called Storax) is choice and desirable, especially suitable for today's gardens. It is native to China and Japan.

USES  As a specimen in situations similar to those suitable for Flowering Dogwood; as an accent and background shrub in large mixed shrub borders, especially those devoted to Rhododendrons, Azaleas, and other broad-leaved evergreens and flowering shrubs; in open woodland or naturalistic areas among tall-growing trees; also on gentle slopes or banks.

HABIT OF GROWTH  Usually several-stemmed, becoming treelike with high, horizontal branches. Eventual height is about 18 feet, although in mild areas it may finally reach 30 feet or so. Lower-growing shrubs like Rhododendrons may be grouped near its base, the Snowbell providing a canopy of light shade.

FLOWERS  Fragrant white flowers, bell-shaped, 1 inch across, in drooping clusters at the ends of short twigs all along the branches, in late spring (June) after the leaves have unfolded.

FOLIAGE  Alternate, oval leaves about 3 inches long that do not hide the flowers.

ASSETS  Showy flowers, pleasantly scented, and attractive plant habit. Blooms when young.

FAULTS  This shrub needs space to assume its natural form, which is rather spreading. Tips may winterkill in severe winter.

CULTURE  Place in areas protected from strong wind, in acid, well-drained soil full of humus. Add peat moss to soil mixture when planting. Do not prune except to remove winterkilled twigs, if any.

# *JETBEAD*

TYPE Deciduous
FAMILY *Rosaceae* (Roz-*ay*-see-ee)
GENUS *Rhodotypos* (Roh-doh-*tye*-pos)
SPECIES *scandens* (*skand*-enz)
ZONE 6

Jetbead is also called White-kerria, after Kerria, which it somewhat resembles. It is native to China and Japan. There is just the one species which has been known from time to time as *Rhodotypos kerrioides* and *tetrapetala,* but in any case, it's the same plant.

USES  A pretty shrub that blends well with others, in foreground of borders or groupings. It will grow in light shade.

HABIT OF GROWTH  Upright, rather stiff, dark brown branches, twigs green, to 6 feet or less, the general effect being airy and graceful.

FLOWERS  Pretty, single white flowers with four petals, about 2 inches across, at the ends of the green twigs; in mid-May principally, but appearing intermittently through the summer. The fruits that follow each bloom are four hard, shining black seeds, prominent and showy.

FOLIAGE  Attractive opposite leaves, about 4 inches long, long-pointed and toothed, darker green on the upper surface, lighter and hairy on the under. The leaves last well into fall.

ASSETS  Versatility in landscaping, effective flowers and fruit, hardiness, medium size.

FAULTS  A blending shrub rather than a star performer. There may be more worthwhile plants for the small property.

CULTURE  Easy to grow in well-drained, average soil, in full sun or light shade. Plants can be cut back to the ground in early spring to make more compact growth.

# KERRIA

TYPE Deciduous
FAMILY *Rosaceae* (Roz-*ay*-see-ee)
GENUS *Kerria* (*Kehr*-ee-uh)
SPECIES *japonica* (jap-*pon*-ik-uh)
ZONE 6

This pretty shrub, overplanted in many areas yet neglected in others, can be very worthwhile in the right setting. It is native to China.

USES  Best planted in groups of three or more (the double-flowered form can stand alone) in the foreground of shrub borders; in certain foundation groupings; and as underplantings in naturalistic or woodland areas. Also against walls and fences of such texture and color as to contrast with the bright-green coloring of the stems and twigs in winter.

HABIT OF GROWTH  Upright, spreading by suckers, with slender, graceful stems to about 4 feet; the double-flowered form is slightly taller. Stems and twigs are bright green in all seasons. There is a variety whose branches are striped green and yellow, but it seems to be rare in nurseries.

FLOWERS  Single yellow flowers with five petals, about 2 inches across, borne singly at the ends of twigs, in mid-spring (and to June in the case of the double-flowered variety). The double Kerria, variety FLORE PLENO, has flowers like small Roses which are longer lasting than the single blooms. Both single and double flowers are illustrated here.

FOLIAGE  Alternate, long-pointed, oval leaves, darker green above, the under surface lighter and somewhat hairy. The leaves have prominent veins and turn yellow in the fall.

ASSETS  A good-natured shrub, bright in flower and an attractive filler later, making an interesting, colorful silhouette in winter. It grows well in light shade. Easy to transplant.

FAULTS  May partially winterkill and thus require spring pruning. Renewal pruning—removal of old stems to the base—may be necessary to revitalize plants.

CULTURE  Grow in average, well-drained soils, in light shade for the single Kerria, whose flowers may fade in bright sun.

# KOREAN ABELIA-LEAF

TYPE Deciduous
FAMILY *Oleaceae* (Oh-lee-*ay*-see-ee)
GENUS *Abeliophyllum* (Ab-beel-ee-oh-*fill*-lum)
SPECIES *distichum* (*diss*-tik-cum)
ZONE 5

Discovered in 1919 in Korea, the Abelia-leaf, or White-forsythia as some are calling this shrub, just goes to prove how slow can be the process of getting a new shrub to the public's attention. Abeliophyllum has found its way to England, where it blooms in February and where no doubt it was noticed by a few sharp-eyed American nurserymen who are now offering it here. It should grow well where the Forsythia grows.

USES   As a specimen or companion to Forsythia in the shrub border and against evergreens or any contrasting background that will accent its lovely flowers.

HABIT OF GROWTH   Slender, arching branches with dark brown bark, reaching about 3 to 4 feet. It is considered very slow growing.

FLOWERS   Fragrant, white flowers, preceded by purple buds produced in the fall, and resembling the bell-shaped flowers of the Forsythia. The flowers, which appear in early spring—in February in mild climates—crowd the stems and show up well against the brown bark.

FOLIAGE   It appears after the flowers. Each leaf is bluish-green, opposite and pointed. The Abeliophyllum may be considered somewhat more attractive than the Forsythia out of bloom.

ASSETS   First, its fragrant, early flowers of great charm, secondly, its neat and slow-growing habit. Some gardeners will be impressed by its rarity.

FAULTS   The fact that its flower buds are susceptible to injury from late spring freezes is surely a black mark against this otherwise most desirable flowering shrub.

CULTURE   Abelia-leaf needs well-drained soil and a location that is sunny and as protected as possible. With such care, chances are good that its flowers will not be injured most winters. (It has been growing in the Morton Arboretum at Lisle, Illinois, since the late 1930s.)

PRUNING  Little should be necessary as the shrub is so slow growing. Fortunately, the branches are not harmed even when the flower buds may be injured.

# KOUSA DOGWOOD

TYPE Deciduous
FAMILY *Cornaceae* (Korn-*nay*-see-ee)
GENUS *Cornus* (*Korn*-us)
SPECIES *kousa* (*koo*-suh)
ZONE 5

The best-known Flowering Dogwood is a tree, *Cornus florida.* (Its Pacific Northwest counterpart is *C. Nuttalli.*) Similar to both is the Kousa Dogwood, from China, considered both a shrubby tree or a treelike shrub, but in either case, choice and beautiful. (Among other Dogwoods are the Bunchberry and the Cornelian-cherry, which see. Other Dogwood species make useful ornamentals, especially those with red, yellow, or bright-green bark in winter, but generally their flowering and fruiting effect is minor and their best use is in naturalistic, semi-wild settings. The best of these are listed in nursery catalogues.)

USES   As a lawn specimen; near a terrace or at boundary corners; also as occasional background accents in mixed shrub borders or at the edge of woodlands or naturalistic areas. Where space is no problem, use the Kousa Dogwood as a hedge, as a planting to outline a drive, or in front of evergreen Pines or Hemlocks.

HABIT OF GROWTH   Single- or multi-stemmed, upright but broad; branch habit tends to be horizontal. Mature specimens can reach 20 feet or so, although 10 feet by 10 feet is the usual size the home gardener can count on.

FLOWERS   After the leaves are developed, tiny flowers in clusters along the upper sides of branches, made showy (as in Bunchberry and Flowering Dogwood) by surrounding white bracts. The bracts of Kousa Dogwood differ from those of Flowering Dogwood by being narrow and pointed and at first creamy white, turning to pink. Blooming time is June, or a good three weeks after Flowering Dogwood. Large Strawberrylike fruits, ½ to 1 inch across, follow, and are eaten by birds.

FOLIAGE   Bright green leaves, about 4 inches long, which turn red in the fall and usually clothe branches densely from top to bottom.

ASSETS   A shrub or small tree for all seasons, especially attractive in its flowering and fruiting stages. It is hardy and easy.

FAULTS  Only possible objection to Kousa Dogwood is its size, which might rule it out for very small properties.

CULTURE  It is a non-demanding plant, hardy to 10 degrees below zero. Planting in early spring is preferable to fall planting. It flowers best in full sun but can be grown in light shade.

# LEATHERWOOD

TYPE Deciduous and evergreen
FAMILY *Cyrillaceae* (Sihr-il-*lay*-see-ee)
GENUS *Cyrilla* (Sihr-*ril*-luh)
SPECIES *racemiflora* (ras-em-if-*floh*-ruh)
ZONE 6

The Leatherwood is charming in flower but is rarely seen in gardens today. It is also called Southern Leatherwood and is native over a wide area from Virginia to Florida, the West Indies and eastern South America.

USES  As a background shrub for borders in mild climates, in open woodland, or as a specimen. In the North it can be colonized in moist woodlands or in shrub borders.

HABIT OF GROWTH  It may eventually reach 25 feet in mild climates, but it is comparatively slow growing and in the North remains at about 5 feet or less. The name Leatherwood comes from the flexibility of the gray-colored twigs and stems.

FLOWERS  Slender, pendulous racemes, 4 to 5 inches long, of small white flowers arranged like those of the Lily-of-the-valley, which come from the base of new growth. They are profuse enough to be very showy and appear in late June and July in the vicinity of New York.

FOLIAGE  Attractive, bright green leaves, alternate, about 2 to 3 inches long. In the North, where Leatherwood is deciduous, leaves turn bright orange and red before falling. In warm climates the leaves are evergreen or semi-evergreen.

ASSETS  Interesting floral effect in early summer.

FAULTS  Straggly growth unless the plants are grown in moist soil and occasionally cut back.

CULTURE  Although native to warm climates, the Leatherwood will endure temperatures to 10 degrees below zero. It must be grown in a humusy, moist soil that is acid. When planting, add peat moss or leafmold to soil mixture. It grows best in light, open shade.

PRUNING  In early spring, when necessary, cut back or shorten straggly stems to keep the plants compact.

# *LEUCOTHOE*

TYPE Broad-leaved evergreen
FAMILY *Ericaceae* (Ehr-ik-*kay*-see-ee)
GENUS *Leucothoe* (Lew-*koth*-oh-ee)
SPECIES *axillaris* (ax-il-*lay*-riss), *Catesbaei* (*Kayts*-bee-eye),
*keiskei* (*kees*-keye)
ZONE 5

A gem of an evergreen for the correct situation. There are Leucothoe species native to North America as well as to Japan.

USES   Best in groups of three or more as foreground or under-planting in naturalistic and shaded areas with Rhododendrons, Flowering Dogwood, Sour-wood, etc. Also suitable for foundation plantings. The foliage is excellent for cutting, to be arranged either alone or mixed with other plant material.

HABIT OF GROWTH   Generally compact, graceful shrubs to 3 or 4 feet, with arching, dark-red stems.

FLOWERS   Waxy, white, slightly fragrant flowers, bell-shaped, in hanging racemes from 3 to 4 inches long; strung along the undersides of the shoots in late spring.

FOLIAGE   Very handsome, alternate leaves, leathery, dark green, slender and pointed. Fall coloring of Drooping Leucothoe (*L. Catesbaei*) may be bronze or dark red.

ASSETS   Attractive foliage and flowers, then Leucothoe's toler-ance of shade and its value as a ground cover of medium height in front of other, more leggy plants. It certainly belongs in any naturalistic planting of acid-soil plants.

FAULTS   It needs acid soil and the foliage will burn in the winter in exposed situations.

CULTURE   It thrives in light or medium shade, in an acid soil full of humus, well drained but able to retain moisture. When planting, add a quantity of leafmold or peat moss to the planting hole. Best effect comes from grouping three to five plants rather than from planting as a specimen. Plants are easy to transplant and also to collect from the wild.

PRUNING   Occasional removal of old stems at the base will force vigorous, compact growth. When leaves are unsightly from winter burn and stems have partially died, part of the plant, or the entire plant, can be cut off at ground level in the spring, and new shoots will arise. When cutting old plants back drastically, mulch with leafmold, compost, and, if available, old, rotted manure.

SPECIES AND VARIETIES  *Leucothoe axillaris.* Coast Leucothoe. Native from Virginia to Florida and Mississippi, so slightly less hardy than *L. Catesbaei,* to which it is otherwise similar. It may be more vigorous, and its foliage does not change color in autumn.

*L. Catesbaei.* Drooping Leucothoe. Native in woods from Virginia to Georgia and Tennessee, but root-hardy to 20 degrees below zero. Best-known species, with several varieties; one is more compact COMPACTA, and another, RAINBOW, has variegated foliage in yellow, pink, red, green.

*L. keiskei.* Keisk's Leucothoe. Native to Japan. Lower growing— to 9 inches. A good ground cover, with showy flowers.

# LILAC

TYPE Deciduous
FAMILY *Oleaceae* (Oh-lee-*ay*-see-ee)
GENUS *Syringa* (Sihr-*ring*-guh)
SPECIES *chinensis* (chin-*nen*-siss), *laciniata* (las-in-ee-*ay*-tuh),
*Meyeri* (*Mye*-er-eye), *microphylla* (mye-kroh-*fill*-uh), *persica*
(*per*-sik-uh), *swegiflexa* (sweh-jee-*flex*-uh), *velutina* (vel-yew-
*tye*-nuh), *villosa* (vil-*loh*-suh), *vulgaris* (vul-*gay*-riss)
ZONE 3, 4, 5

If sentiment alone determined the most popular flowering shrub, it might well be the Lilac. There is hardly a person whose memory is not stirred by it, and its scent is one of the most familiar of all perfumes associated with flowers. While the Lilac is not a native, it was one of the first plants brought by early settlers and has become so widely naturalized as to appear a native. Lilacs originate in Asia and Europe. The so-called French Lilacs are hybrids of the Common Lilac (*Syringa vulgaris*), many of which were introduced by Victor Lemoine. While named varieties of Lilac are strikingly beautiful, there are species available which can be useful in contemporary gardens.

USES  Gardeners today may have space for only one or two Lilacs and must leave the bordering of walks and drives with different Lilacs to parks and arboretums. (For gardeners who *do* have space, collecting Lilacs can be delightful and planting a Lilac Walk or a hedge of Lilacs around a large vegetable garden are both ideal ways to use and enjoy them.) A few Lilacs can be used in the background of a mixed shrub border; where space between properties is generous, they can be planted as a hedge. Probably their best use today is for occasional use around properties—as a specimen off the corner of a house (they are much too tall and spreading for foundations and, alas, for most doorways), as a corner planting near a terrace, or against high walls or fences. Those who appreciate Lilacs can always find room for a couple! As every flower arranger knows, Lilacs are stunning in arrangements. When Lilac blooms wilt after being cut, try peeling some bark off the stem ends, plunge them deeply into hot water, and leave until they perk up.

HABIT OF GROWTH  Varieties and hybrids of the Common Lilac are upright, usually with several stems unless trained otherwise, and tend to form thickets by suckering freely. Eventually plants may reach 9 to 20 feet, although proper pruning can help to keep Lilacs from reaching the second story. Some of the species form rounded, shrubby plants, usually between 6 and 9 feet in height.

**FLOWERS** Most varieties of the Common Lilac—but not all —are deliciously fragrant. Fragrance among the species differs in appeal and intensity. All Lilacs have small tubular flowers, single or double, and, in the case of most hybrids and named varieties, carried in showy panicles, usually cone-shaped and 10 or more inches long. The species often display their flowers more informally, in shorter panicles, but in such quantities as to cover the bush. Lilac Time is usually mid-spring, that is from early May to early June, depending on the season as well as the region and the particular plant involved.

**FOLIAGE** Opposite leaves, usually dark green and shiny, and fully developed before the flowers open.

**ASSETS** Very showy flowers, usually sweetly fragrant, as well as hardiness (most Lilacs will endure very low winter temperatures). Beyond some annual pruning and occasional spraying, Lilacs are easy to grow and care for.

**FAULTS** For year-round landscape value, the Lilac does not offer much. There is also the fact that in general they are vigorous and wide-spreading by nature and thus not suited to many small properties.

**CULTURE** Grow in full sun, in well-drained average soil. Plant in spring or fall—Lilacs are easy to transplant. Lilacs do better in neutral or slightly alkaline soils, but often perform very satisfactorily in acid-soil regions. In fact, Lilacs can be grown fairly near Azaleas and other acid-soil lovers if spot applications of limestone or wood ashes are made to the Lilacs. When ordering Lilacs, try to obtain "own-root" rather than grafted plants. Grafted Lilacs can be set 3 to 4 inches deeper than they were in the nursery to encourage the forming of new roots. (Lilacs are usually grafted on Privet and naturally any Privet shoots noticed at the base of the plant should be removed.) Lilac plants need a few years to flower. After that, when flowers do not appear, try digging a trench around the base of the bush, mixing a generous amount of superphosphate (8 oz. to 3 feet of ditch). Lime may bring plants to bloom if soil is very acid and lime has not been previously applied. Overfertilizing may cause excessive vegetative growth of the plant at the expense of flowers. An early-spring application of a complete fertilizer is recommended for Lilacs that have been flowering normally. Top-dressing with rotted manure, when available, or compost, is recommended. When planting a Lilac hedge, set the plants 3 feet apart.

PESTS AND DISEASES   Lilacs are susceptible to *mildew,* especially when in light shade. It does no harm and is hardly worth trying to control. *Stem borers* sometimes invade mature stems, and can be detected by the entrance holes near the base of the plants. Cut off such infested stems just below the hole and destroy. An aerosol spray is available for controlling borers in Lilacs, Dogwoods, etc. Occasionally the *Lilac scale* appears— to control, spray in late winter or early spring with a miscible oil spray.

PRUNING   Remove suckers that come up at base of plant, leaving only a few to take the place of older stems cut off every three years or so to keep plants bushy and not too tall. Remove flower heads of varieties and hybrids right after they fade. To rejuvenate very old Lilac plants, a three-year program is recommended by Dr. Donald Wyman of the Arnold Arboretum, where many Lilacs are grown. The first year cut one third of the branches back to the ground; the second year cut back another third, and the third year, the remaining ones. In the Lilac species, prune as necessary to shape the plants, removing old and weak stems after flowering.

SPECIES AND VARIETIES   *Syringa chinensis.* (Also listed as *S. rothomagensis*). A hybrid between *S. persica* and *S. vulgaris.* Graceful, slender shrub, to 10 feet. Flowers, purple-lilac or white, in loose panicles in May. Zone 3.
*S. laciniata.* Cutleaf Lilac or Cutleaf Persian Lilac. Native to Turkestan and China. Considered very choice. Its dainty lavender flower clusters, very fragrant, cover the slender branches in late May. Zone 6.

*S. Meyeri.* Meyer's Lilac. Rare, choice species from China, a favorite of Montague Free's. Neat shrub to 5 or 6 feet, bearing many dainty clusters of lilac-colored flowers in May. Zone 3.

*S. microphylla.* Littleleaf Lilac. Very spreading shrub only 6 feet tall. Native to China. Bears small panicles of very scented lilac-pink flowers in late May or early June. Its buds are dark red. Sometimes it flowers again in the fall. Zone 4.

*S. persica.* Persian Lilac. One of the best Lilacs, probably of hybrid origin. Slender, graceful habit, reaching a height of 6 to 7 feet, and ultimately wide spreading. Profuse, yet delicate clusters of spicily fragrant, pale lilac flowers in late May, early June. There is a white variety. Zone 5. The so-called Cutleaf Persian Lilac, according to Dr. Donald Wyman of Harvard's Arnold Arboretum, is *S. laciniata,* which is listed above.

*S. swegiflexa.* Pink Pearl Lilac. Hybrid between *S. sweginzowi* and *S. reflexa.* Neat shrub up to 6 or 7 feet, bearing long panicles of pink flowers in June which are very fragrant. The flower buds are deep red. Valued for its late bloom. Zone 6.

*S. velutina.* Dwarf Korean Lilac. Also listed as *S. palibiniana.* Super-hardy Lilac from Korea which has a great future. Slow-growing but may reach 6 feet. Its lavender flowers are borne on 6-inch panicles in June. MISS KIM is a selection having late-flowering lilac-purple flowers which fade to almost white and long, waxy leaves which turn burgundy red in the fall. Zone 4, perhaps Zone 3.

*S. villosa.* Very hardy species from China, sometimes called the Late Lilac. Its dense panicles of rosy-lilac flowers appear in June. It has large oblong leaves 7 inches long. The PRESTON hybrids, developed in Canada by Miss Isabella Preston of the Canadian Experimental Station, are selections of crosses between *S. villosa* and *S. reflexa.* JAMES MACFARLAND is a seedling with *S. villosa* blood and is worth noting for its super hardiness, late blooming (well into June around New York), and clear pink color. Zone 3.

*S. vulgaris.* Common Lilac. Native to southeastern Europe, this is the Lilac that everyone knows. Some assume it is native because it is so often seen in deserted areas, a final reminder that the area was once occupied—and planted—by man. It has fragrant lavender or white flowers in May, often carried far up on branches that make the plants seem more like trees than shrubs. It suckers freely and if unchecked forms wide thickets. Zone 3. It is this Lilac, also, that is responsible for the term "French Hybrid" or "French Lilac," probably because many originated in France. There are many, many varieties, only a few of which can be listed here (consult catalogues for descriptions). ALICE EASTWOOD (red-purple); EDITH CAVELL (creamy white); CHARLES JOLY (double red); MARECHAL FOCH (bright rose); PAUL THIRION (reddish lavender-blue); PRIMROSE (pale yellow); VESTALE (single white); BELLE DE NANCY (satiny pink).

# *MAHONIA*

TYPE Evergreen
FAMILY *Berberidaceae* (Ber-ber-id-*day*-see-ee)
GENUS *Mahonia* (Mah-*hoh*-nee-uh)
SPECIES *aquifolium* (ak-kwi-*foh*-lee-um), *Bealei* (*Beel*-ee-eye),
*Lomariaefolia* (Loh-mah-ree-ee-*foh*-lee-uh), *repens* (*ree*-penz)
ZONE See descriptions of species, below

The most common of the Mahonias is the Oregon Holly-grape, *Mahonia aquifolium,* native to parts of our Pacific Northwest, and very handsome it can be when conditions suit it. The Mahonias are close relatives to the Barberry, a connection more apparent when Mahonia is compared with the evergreen Barberries.

USES Attractive foliage plants for shade in the North, in foundations or in foreground of mixed shrub borders, especially with Rhododendrons. Creeping Mahonia (*M. repens*) is an effective ground cover. Most of the Mahonia species should be planted in groups rather than as specimens. *Mahonia Bealei* is singular enough in appearance to be used as a specimen for accent, especially against walls around contemporary homes where its stiff, rather exotic habit does not look out of place.

HABIT OF GROWTH Generally upright and broad, suckering plants with dense foliage.

FLOWERS Small, yellow flower clusters in tight racemes from 3 to 6 inches long, at the ends of branches in early to mid-spring (usually early May). Some are fragrant. The flowers are followed by bunches of Grapelike, dark blue berries in summer.

FOLIAGE Evergreen, compound leaves composed of several leaflets, each from 2½ to 5 inches long (depending on species), of a leathery texture and spiny like a Holly. Color varies from dark green to blue-green.

ASSETS Handsome plants in foliage, flowers and fruit, useful because they prefer some shade and are responsive to pruning. They are tolerant of average, even poor, soil. In the moist, cool Northwest they are superb.

FAULTS In the North, Mahonia does not always take dry, severe cold well, its foliage often ending up the winter marred by scorch. Mahonia shouldn't be planted if a site sheltered from winter wind and sun can't be provided, and if the gardener is unwilling to practice maintenance pruning necessary to remove dead foliage and to keep the plants compact and shapely.

CULTURE Mahonia will grow in sun or part shade in average soil in mild, moist climates. Elsewhere protection from winter sun and wind is necessary—a northeast exposure, for example, would provide sun protection. It thrives in a variety of well-drained soils—sandy, stony, or humusy. It will respond to a quantity of peat moss mixed in its hole at planting time as well as to an annual spring fertilizing with any general-purpose fertilizer.

PRUNING Prune after flowering to remove winter-burned branches. (Early spring pruning is satisfactory, too, but in most cases would cut off flowering buds.) Stems can be cut off at ground level if they have become leggy; otherwise prune where desired to maintain shape and height. Mahonia tolerates drastic pruning, as it spreads by suckers.

SPECIES *Mahonia aquifolium.* Oregon Holly-grape. Native to Pacific Northwest and suitable for Zone 5 where winter temperatures do not fall below 10 degrees below zero. Height, about 3 feet. Foliage shiny, bronze in fall, very susceptible to winter burn in the North unless protected from drying winds. Prune after the showy yellow flowers have appeared.
*M. Bealei.* Leatherleaf Mahonia. Native to China. Less hardy than the Oregon Holly-grape but suitable for Zone 7 or regions where winter temperatures do not go below zero. This species can reach 12 feet; it needs careful placement because of its stiff, rather exotic appearance. Foliage is evergreen, dull, with year-round bronze cast; it is composed of nine to fifteen rigid leaflets, 5 inches long. Yellow flower clusters are very showy and fragrant.
*M. Lomariaefolia.* Chinese Holly-grape. Native to China. Suitable for warmer, protected parts of Zone 8 where temperature remains above 20 degrees. Stiff, tropical-appearing plant, its compound leaves arranged horizontally to form a striking pattern. Much used on West Coast. Yellow flowers are very showy.
*M. repens.* Creeping Mahonia. Native to Pacific Northwest. Hardy to 10 degrees below zero. Height, about 1 foot. Similar to Oregon Holly-grape, and while useful as a ground cover and recommended for general planting, it is rarely carried by nurseries.

# MEXICAN-ORANGE

TYPE Evergreen
FAMILY *Rutaceae* (Roo-*tay*-see-ee)
GENUS *Choisya* (*Koy*-see-uh)
SPECIES *ternata* (ter-*nay*-tah)
ZONE 8

Choice for the South and mild-climate gardens of the West Coast is the Mexican-orange, native to Mexico.

USES   Handsome near entrances and doorways, against walls and fences, and as a tub plant. In the North, it can be grown in greenhouses.

HABIT OF GROWTH   Rounded, dense bush, to about 6 feet.

FLOWERS   White, starry flowers, with a Hawthorn scent, in clusters at the ends of shoots and from leaf axils, in early spring and often intermittently thereafter.

FOLIAGE   Attractive trifoliate leaves which are glossy and evergreen.

ASSETS   Its attractive, scented flowers, handsome foliage and neat form.

FAULTS   Flowers can be injured by frost when grown in the extremes of its climate range.

CULTURE   Grow in full sun in well-drained, light but humusy soil, in a position protected from strong winds. It needs little pruning other than that for the purpose of training if grown against walls or in other special locations. Occasionally, old plants can be thinned at the base—after flowering.

# *MOCK-ORANGE*

TYPE Deciduous
FAMILY *Saxifragaceae* (Sax-if-rag-*gay*-see-ee)
GENUS *Philadelphus* (Fil-ad-*delf*-us)
SPECIES *coronarius* (kor-oh-*nay*-ree-us), *cymosus* (sye-*moh*-sus),
*Lemoinei* (Lew-*moyn*-ee-eye), *virginalis* (vir-jin-*nay*-liss)
ZONE 4 and 5

Perhaps the best-named flowering shrub is the Mock-orange, as both its pure white flowers and delightful fragrance are reminiscent of true Orange blossoms. However, there are scentless species and varieties of Mock-orange, although none are listed here. In fact, the known list of Philadelphus species, hybrids and varieties is a vast one and many botanical gardens and arboretums—the Arnold Arboretum, for one—have assembled them. Although today's home gardens have space for only one or two—a shrub border without Mock-orange, even though the flower display lasts only a few weeks—is a poor thing. There are species native to North America as well as Europe and Asia, and much of the hybridizing was done in France by the famous plant breeder Victor Lemoine.

USES   In the shrub border, both as background or farther-front subjects or as part of smaller shrub groupings. Also as informal hedges or screens. A few make suitable specimens, but unfortunately their flowers are scentless or they are not easily available. Cut branches can make a scented bouquet for indoors.

HABIT OF GROWTH   Bushy, upright, rounded plants with dense foliage. On some the branches may arch or droop. Heights range from a few feet to 10 feet or more.

FLOWERS   Single or double flowers, usually clustered along the branches, white and usually very fragrant. There are a few yellow, rose, or purple-tinted flowers. Flowering time is late spring.

FOLIAGE   Opposite leaves, sometimes soft and grayish. A few species offer golden-leaved variations.

ASSETS   The pure white, scented flowers, borne in great profusion and covering the bush. They are hardy and easy to grow.

FAULTS   Not much distinction out of bloom.

CULTURE   Grow in full sun or very light shade in well-drained average soil that retains moisture. Add peat moss to planting hole. Mock-orange blooms on old wood, so prune after flowering. Don't shear Mock-orange like a Privet—if it outgrows its spot, transplant in early spring or discard and get a more compact variety. Every few years, cut back a few of the oldest stems at ground level to maintain vitality. Otherwise, Mock-orange needs little care.

SPECIES AND VARIETIES  *Philadelphus coronarius.* Native to Europe and southwest Asia; its single flowers, about 1½ inches across, are very fragrant. There is a yellow-leaved variety, AUREA. Height about 9 feet.

*P. cymosus.* Hybrid and parent of VOIE LACTEE, large, single flowers; CONQUETE, white single flowers, very fragrant.

*P. Lemoinei.* Hybrid, with *P. coronarius* as a parent. Named varieties include ATLAS, very large single flowers 3 inches across; BELLE ETOILE, single white; GIRANDOLE, of compact habit, with double flowers; INNOCENCE, double and very fragrant; BOULE D'ARGENT, double flowers; OCHROLEUCUS, low-growing with creamy white, semi-double flowers; and many others.

*P. virginalis.* Also a Lemoine hybrid. Varieties include the popular VIRGINAL, clusters of double, very scented white flowers; MINNESOTA SNOWFLAKE, double flowers; GLACIER, double flowers; BOUQUET BLANC, moundlike, slow growth. Other Mock-orange hybrids available and worthwhile include: BEAUCLERK, large, fragrant flowers with a purple tint at their base on plant with arching, graceful habit, to 6 feet; ENCHANTMENT, double flowers, very fragrant, and upright habit, to 6 feet; SILVER SHOWERS, dwarf to 3 feet, with single flowers; FROSTY MORN, dwarf to 4 feet, with double flowers.

# MOUNTAIN-LAUREL

TYPE Broad-leaved evergreen
FAMILY *Ericaceae* (Ehr-ik-*ay*-see-ee)
GENUS *Kalmia* (*Kal*-mee-uh)
SPECIES *angustifolia* (an-gus-tif-*foh*-lee-uh), *latifolia* (lat-if-*foh*-lee-uh), *polifolia* (pol-if-*foh*-lee-uh)
ZONE 4

North America can well be proud of this beautiful native shrub. It is a common sight in untouched woodlands, mountains and hillsides from New Brunswick and central New Hampshire to northern Florida and west to Tennessee, Ohio, and Indiana, and is a popular plant for landscaped parkways and state highways. Two other species of *Kalmia,* less familiar, are the Sheep-laurel and Bog-laurel, described at the end of this section.

USES   Think of Mountain-laurel first when there is a shade problem, either on the north side of a house or garage, or under tall trees like Oaks, or as evergreen accents in any woodland area that is to remain naturalistic. However, don't rule out the Mountain-laurel from sunny locations where it can get sufficient water. Use it in shrub borders or groupings as a companion to Azaleas and Rhododendrons, and with Flowering Dogwoods and other small trees. It makes an excellent covering for a bank or slope.

HABIT OF GROWTH   Nursery-grown plants are usually compact and bushy and may reach a height of 4 to 8 feet, although in the wild the plants are more often found in thickets. Some ancient plants are more treelike in height and trunk growth.

FLOWERS   The pink-and-white flowers, about ¾ inch across, appear in rounded clusters at the ends of branches in late May or June in New England, earlier southward. To fully appreciate the magnificence of the Mountain-laurel in bloom, one should see it in the Great Smoky Mountains National Park in Tennessee in May and in other areas where it is protected in its native state.

FOLIAGE   Handsome, evergreen leaves, alternate and about 5 inches long.

ASSETS   This shrub has everything—good form, good foliage and superb flowers borne in abundance. It is handsome in and out of flower and combines well with other trees and shrubs. Given the right soil (see below) it is easy to grow.

FAULTS Foliage may burn during the winter in windy, exposed situations. It is also susceptible to a disfiguring leaf-spot disease.

CULTURE Mountain-laurel must have an acid, moist soil. Beyond that requirement, it grows under a variety of conditions. The home gardener should mix peat moss and leafmold in the planting hole and then keep plants mulched with Oak leaves, Pine needles. Plants do best when they receive plenty of moisture. Mountain-laurel makes its best growth in semi-shade, although it can be expected to do well in full shade or sun. No pruning is necessary, although those who collect plants from the wild may find they are leggy and need to have their taller branches cut back. New, bushy growth, more compact, will then arise. Plants of Mountain-laurel are easily increased by seed sown indoors in early winter in pure sphagnum moss which is kept moist under a covering of polyethylene. Seedlings can be set out in spring in a sand-peat soil mixture and must be shaded.

PESTS AND DISEASES There is a leaf-spot disease which can be controlled by spraying with ferbam or zineb in the spring and repeating twice at intervals of two weeks. Another disease, a blight, causes large purple-brown spots on the leaves. The control is the same as for the leaf spot.

SPECIES *Kalmia latifolia.* Mountain-laurel or Calico-bush. Described above.
*K. angustifolia.* Sheep-laurel, Lamb-kill. Of interest to collectors of native plants and to those who collect acid-soil plants. Rosy flowers in late spring, miniature versions of Mountain-laurel's, but less showy. Its straggly growth may reach 2 to 4 feet. Its evergreen leaves, about 2½ inches long, are blue-green above, paler underneath.
*K. polifolia.* Bog-laurel, Swamp-laurel, Bog-kalmia. This 2-foot relative ranges from the Northeast to Colorado and California; it is found in bogs and in the mountains. It has rosy-purple flowers, considered attractive, in early summer.

# NEILLIA

TYPE Deciduous
FAMILY *Rosaceae* (Roz-*ay*-see-ee)
GENUS *Neillia* (*Neel*-ee-uh)
SPECIES *longiracemosa* (lon-jih-ray-sem-*moh*-suh), *sinensis* (sin-*nen*-siss)
ZONE 6

Pretty shrubs, related to Spirea and Stephanandra, too rarely seen in modern gardens. Both species are native to China.

USES  Toward the front of shrub groupings or borders, or as accents in flower gardens.

HABIT OF GROWTH  Graceful, arching shrub, its slender, irregularly branched stems reaching 3 to 5 feet. Stems have red-brown color.

FLOWERS  Small, bell-shaped flowers, white or pink, in racemes 2 to 3 inches long at the ends of branches, in late spring (late May and June).

FOLIAGE  Alternate, toothed or lobed leaves, 2 to 4 inches long, attractive and lacy in effect.

ASSETS  Essentially desirable flowering shrubs, of special interest to the collector and plantsman.

FAULTS  Little known, little grown and not generally available.

CULTURE  Easy to grow and to transplant. Best in very light shade and well-drained, moist but average soil. When planting, add organic matter. In northern areas, top growth may winter-kill; prune back to live wood in early spring.

SPECIES  *Neillia longiracemosa*. Native to China. Rose-pink flowers in late May and June. Height 3 to 5 feet. Considered choice.
*N. sinensis*. Native to China. White or pale pink flowers in late May to June. Height ultimately about 6 feet.

# OCEAN SPRAY

TYPE Deciduous
FAMILY *Rosaceae* (Roz-*ay*-see-ee)
GENUS *Holodiscus* (Hol-oh-*disk*-us)
SPECIES *discolor* (dis-*kol*-or)
ZONE 5

Ocean Spray, Rock-spirea, and Cream-bush are samples of the descriptive names given to this Western American native. It is found from British Columbia to California as well as in Idaho and Montana, and will survive winter temperatures to 20 degrees below zero; so there is no reason why it should not be grown in the Midwest and East. It was once known as *Spirea discolor*.

USES  Probably best planted in groups of three or more plants in a mixed shrub border, especially against dark backgrounds or darker-foliaged shrubs so that its creamy flowers stand out.

HABIT OF GROWTH  Slender branches, loose, and arching when in bloom; 5 to 6 feet long. Each shrub eventually sends up many stems to form a bushy, spreading plant.

FLOWERS  Fluffy panicles, 8 inches long, of creamy white flowers in July, heavy enough to arch the branches gracefully.

FOLIAGE  Alternate, broad leaves, 4 inches long, hairy and gray underneath.

ASSETS  Its early- to midsummer flowering period, as well as the showy flowers themselves.

FAULTS  Although it is hardly to be blamed on the Ocean Spray (it is better known in England than in its native America!), it is listed by few nurseries and is reputed to be difficult to move from the wild.

CULTURE  The Ocean Spray will grow in sun or very light shade and prefers a rich, humusy soil. When planting, mix peat moss, compost, or any other organic matter on hand, into the soil.

PRUNING  Occasionally some winterkill of branches may occur; when this happens, the dead ends should be cut off in the spring. After flowering, it is recommended that the faded panicles be removed for the sake of neatness.

# OLEANDER

TYPE Evergreen
FAMILY *Apocynaceae* (Ap-oh-syn-*ay*-see-ee)
GENUS *Nerium* (*Neer*-ee-um)
SPECIES *oleander* (oh-lee-*an*-der)
ZONE 8

This southern beauty, familiar to traveling Northerners, is now widely grown in warm areas of the West Coast as well as in the South. It is still a popular tub subject for terraces in the North. The Oleander is native to the Mediterranean area.

USES   As a specimen, as a hedge, or in tubs to decorate terraces.

HABIT OF GROWTH   Erect, slender shrub with several stems unless otherwise restricted, eventually reaching 20 feet. Can be trained to form of small tree with single stem.

FLOWERS   Showy, funnel-shaped flowers, single or double, in clusters at the ends of branches in early spring through the summer. Colors include red, white, rose, salmon, and pink. Some have a pronounced fragrance.

FOLIAGE   Attractive, narrow and leathery, about 8 inches long, of a gray-green cast.

ASSETS   The colorful flowers, plus easy maintenance, make these useful shrubs for mild climates. They are ideal flowering plants for tubs in the North if they can be kept in a cool greenhouse during the cold months. Fragrance of some is a dividend.

FAULTS   Tendency toward legginess.

CULTURE   The Oleander likes full sun and is drought resistant. Root pruning is recommended as a means of keeping the plants from growing too tall. Cutting back the plants in early spring will force new shoots but will reduce flowering. Oleanders are so easy to propagate that cuttings placed in water soon form roots.

VARIETIES   There are several available, including MRS. ROEDING, with double salmon-pink flowers; SEELY PINK, single pink; SISTER AGNES, single white; COMPTE BARTHELEMY, double, bright red.

# PARROTIA

TYPE Deciduous
FAMILY *Hamamelidaceae* (Ham-am-mel-id-*day*-see-ee)
GENUS *Parrotia* (Par-*roh*-tee-uh)
SPECIES *persica* (*per*-sik-ah)
ZONE 6

This shrub or small tree is for the collector as well as the home gardener who has space enough to concentrate on shrubs for early-spring interest. Parrotia is in the Witch-hazel family. It is native to Persia and hardy to 10 degrees below zero.

USES   As background in shrub borders for lower-growing shrubs, or on the outskirts of woodland, or in naturalistic plantings. It can also be used as a specimen, especially where its winter outline will be prominent.

HABIT OF GROWTH   Multi-stemmed, upright growth, eventually to 15 feet, the branches slightly arching. The gray bark flakes off to leave white patches, especially prominent in winter.

FLOWERS   Fuzzy, rusty-brown flowers like those of the Witch-hazels, with prominent stamens, before the foliage, in early spring (late March–April). While the flowers are not eye-stoppers, they do appear without competition of foliage and have a quiet appeal when caught by bright spring sunshine.

FOLIAGE   Alternate, rounded leaves, about 4 inches long, that clothe the branches. They are soft in texture and bright green. In the fall, the foliage turns bright yellow, red, or orange.

ASSETS   A large shrub that improves with age, giving interest in three seasons: early spring for its curious flowers, autumn for its foliage color, winter for its bark patterns.

FAULTS   Parrotia may grow too large for the average small property, and it may not be dramatic enough in flower to suit the taste of all. It is not carried by most nurserymen.

CULTURE   It grows in average, well-drained soil in full sun or light shade. It requires no special pruning and is free from pests and diseases.

# PEARL-BUSH

TYPE Deciduous
FAMILY *Rosaceae* (Roz-*ay*-see-ee)
GENUS *Exochorda* (Ex-oh-*kord*-uh)
SPECIES *Giraldi* (Jir-*all*-dye), *macrantha* (mak-*ranth*-uh), *race-mosa* (ras-em-*moh*-suh)
ZONE 5

The charm of Pearl-bush is in its oval, white flower buds. This Asian native should be better known—it is well suited to modern gardens.

USES   Best as a specimen, either in the background of a shrub border or handled like a small tree (such as Flowering Dogwood), with a few lower-growing shrubs in front of it. However, Pearl-bush THE BRIDE, which grows only about 4 feet high, is an exception; it should be used in the foreground of mixed shrub plantings.

HABIT OF GROWTH   Upright, to about 9 feet, then spreading, making a treelike silhouette. (THE BRIDE, of course, remains low and bushy.)

FLOWERS   Racemes of oval buds like pearls which open to pure white, five-petaled flowers, about 1½ inches across, with a prominent green calyx; in late April or early May.

FOLIAGE   Alternate leaves about 2½ inches long. The petioles are sometimes red.

ASSETS   Attractive buds and flowers which together are very showy.

FAULTS   The plants may seem lanky, but this fault can be covered by planting lower-growing material at their base.

CULTURE   Grow in sun in well-drained soil to which peat moss or other organic material has been added at planting time.

PRUNING   After flowering, to shorten the stems and increase the number of flowers for the following year; prune, too, for training, if necessary.

SPECIES AND VARIETIES  *Exochorda Giraldi.* Native to China. May reach 15 feet. Its leaf petioles are red. Var. *Wilsoni* has larger flowers and more of them.

*E. macrantha.* Hybrid between *E. racemosa* and *E. Korolkowi,* from Turkestan. THE BRIDE variety is very compact, floriferous, and only 4 feet tall. White flowers in early May.

*E. racemosa.* The most commonly planted Pearl-bush, and native to China. Height about 9 feet. Very desirable.

# PHOTINIA

TYPE Deciduous and evergreen
FAMILY *Rosaceae* (Roz-*ay*-see-ee)
GENUS *Photinia* (Foh-*tin*-ee-uh)
SPECIES *serrulata* (ser-rew-*lay*-tuh), *villosa* (vil-*loh*-suh)
ZONE See descriptions of species, below

Borderline in flower value compared to some shrubs, Photinia nevertheless possesses charm when in bloom. Its other good points mark it as a fine plant for modern gardens. Both species are native to Asia.

USES   Best as a specimen. In fact, on a very small property, Photinia can be used as a small tree in situations where the larger Flowering Dogwood might ordinarily be placed. Where space is not a problem, Photinia can be planted as an accent in a large mixed shrub or flower border. Both species are effective against walls, and *P. serrulata* is often espaliered. Both flowers and fruit are effective in arrangements.

HABIT OF GROWTH   Large, upright, eventually like a small tree; to 12 feet high, its head almost as wide.

FLOWERS   Round, flat clusters of small white flowers, about ⅜ inch across, in May; blossoms are similar to a Hawthorn's. They can cover the bush and give an effective, snowy display. The bright red fruits that follow are much showier and are at their best in the fall. They are attractive to birds.

FOLIAGE   Glabrous, toothed, oval leaves which are alternate and about 3 inches long (in the case of *P. villosa*). They sometimes become yellowish in the fall. The leaves of *P. serrulata* are evergreen, very glossy and about 8 inches long. New growth is red or bronze.

ASSETS   Handsome fruiting shrubs with dividends in flowers, foliage and habit.

FAULTS   Both species are large shrubs and are at their best when not crowded.

CULTURE   Full sun, well-drained soil to which peat moss has been added at planting time.

PRUNING   *P. villosa* rarely needs pruning except that indicated for the purpose to which it has been put—to keep its form as a treelike specimen with one trunk, a specimen against a wall, and so on. The Chinese Photinia can have its new growth pinched several times a season to force more new growth with desirable bronze coloring. It can be espaliered.

SPECIES *Photinia serrulata*. Chinese Photinia. From China. Large evergreen shrub or small tree, eventually to 30 feet. Hardy in Zone 7 where temperatures remain above 10 degrees. *P. villosa*. Oriental Photinia, sometimes called Christmas-berry. From Japan, China and Korea. It is hardier than the other species, growing in Zone 5 and withstanding temperatures as low as 20 degrees below zero.

# PRIVET

TYPE Deciduous and evergreen
FAMILY *Oleaceae* (Oh-lee-*ay*-see-ee)
GENUS *Ligustrum* (Lig-*gust*-rum)
SPECIES *amurense* (am-moor-*ren*-see), *Henryi* (*Hen*-ree-eye),
*ibolium* (eye-*boh*-lee-um), *japonicum* (jap-*pon*-ik-um), *lucidum*
(*lew*-sid-um), *obtusifolium* (ob-tew-sif-*foh*-lee-um), *ovalifolium*
(oh-val-if-*foh*-lee-um), *Quihoui* (Kwee-*hoo*-ee), *sinense* (sin-*nen*-
see), *Vicaryi* (Veye-*kar*-ee-eye), *vulgare* (vul-*gay*-ree)
ZONE See descriptions of species, below

Everyone knows the value of Privet for making hedges and screens. Less appreciated are the many spikes of white flowers which cover unclipped plants. While the handsome evergreen species are rated too tender for many northern gardens, one or two have proved to be hardier than thought. The various Privet species are native to Asia and the Mediterranean region.

USES As hedges, sheared or unsheared, kept low or high; as wall plants; as specimens; some as foundation plants; as subjects for mixed shrub borders. Privet can be trained as desired, even as living sculpture. Both the flowers and the berries that follow them can be used in arrangements.

HABIT OF GROWTH Upright, densely branched and twigged, some naturally forming rounded outlines, others becoming open and even treelike with age. Climate as well as the species influences growth patterns of Privet. Heights range from 6 to 8 feet to 15, or even 30, feet.

FLOWERS Small, white or creamy flowers, funnel-shaped, in dense panicles or spikes from a few inches long to 10 inches or more. The flowers are of varying fragrance, sometimes considered too sweet, but generally pleasant and able to permeate the surrounding atmosphere. The black and purple-black berries that follow can be effective, and they also attract birds.

FOLIAGE Privet foliage, in both evergreen and deciduous species, rates very high. Opposite, short-petioled leaves, usually glossy, and, in the evergreen kinds, leathery and thick, with a waxy texture. Several species offer yellow-variegated forms.

ASSETS Adaptability in landscaping—there is a Privet for every climate and use—as well as tolerance of wind, of the unfavorable environment of cities, of salt spray. Some Privets are fast growing, others slow. Beyond pruning and training for special purposes, they require no care and are free from pests and diseases. The fragrant flower spikes and fruit can be showy.

FAULTS When Privet does not perform satisfactorily, it is usually the gardener's fault: for instance, if a hedge becomes open and leggy at its base, it has been pruned incorrectly.

CULTURE Grow in average, well-drained soil in full sun or half shade. Privet is easily increased by the home gardener from softwood cuttings taken in late spring or early summer.

PRUNING Actually little if any is required unless plants are used in formal hedges where regular shearing is essential, usually several times in a growing season. It is important to taper the shape upward from the base, which must be kept wider than the top. This will keep the hedge solidly leafy from base to top, eliminating legginess and bareness. When Privet is grown as an informal hedge, its flowers and fruit can be enjoyed. Necessary pruning can be done after flowering. Evergreen Privets like *Ligustrum japonicum* can be cut back occasionally, but their natural shape is a pleasing, rounded form. Up North these evergreen Privets may suffer winter injury; damaged parts should be cut back to live wood in the spring.

SPECIES AND VARIETIES *Ligustrum amurense*. Amur Privet. White flowers in 2-inch spikes in mid-June, and black berries in fall. Hardy in Zone 4 where temperatures don't go below 20 degrees below zero.
*L. Henryi*. White flowers in 5-inch panicles in August. Its leaves are evergreen, about 2 inches long. Hardy to Zone 7.
*L. ibolium*. Hybrid with small flower spikes. Hardy to Zone 5 where winter temperatures don't regularly fall below 10 degrees below zero.
*L. japonicum*. Japanese Privet. One of the Privet elite, with handsome, glossy evergreen leaves about 3 to 4 inches long and 6-inch flower panicles in early summer. Eventual height about 10 feet but it grows compactly and slowly in the North and can be used in foundation plantings. Hardy to Zone 6. Thrives on Long Island and its range could probably be extended northward, particularly along the coast. Variety SUWANEE RIVER may be somewhat hardier.

*L. lucidum.* Glossy or Waxleaf Privet. Similar to the preceding species and much planted in the South. Its evergreen leaves are larger, up to 6 inches, its flowers in 10-inch panicles. There are several varieties, some with variegated leaves. Becomes tree, to 30 feet, in South. Zone 7, protected areas of Zones 6 and 5.

*L. obtusifolium.* Sometimes listed as *L. ibota.* Height about 10 feet. Flower panicles 1½ inches long, in mid-June. Var. *Regelianum,* the popular Regel Privet, is a choice, low-growing shrub, different from others because of its spreading, horizontal-branching pattern. Remains about 4 to 5 inches high. Hardy to Zone 5.

*L. ovalifolium.* California Privet. Native to Japan. Creamy white flower clusters 4 inches long, in July. Semi-evergreen. Sometimes suffers winter injury in extremes of its zone. Zone 4.

*L. Quihoui.* Outstanding for its late flowers, in 8-inch panicles in September. Deciduous shrub up to 6 feet. Zone 6 or 7. Plant in protected site.

*L. sinense.* Especially floriferous, with white flowers in 4-inch panicles in early summer. Semi-evergreen in North. There is a variegated form. Height 12 feet. Zone 7.

*L. Vicaryi.* Yellow or chartreuse foliage, desirable in special situations. Height 12 feet. Zone 5.

*L. vulgare.* Common Privet. Popular hedge plant. White flowers in early summer. Foliage semi-evergreen. Zone 5.

# PUSSY WILLOW

TYPE Deciduous
FAMILY *Salicaceae* (Say-lee-*kay*-see-ee)
GENUS *Salix* (*Say*-lix)
SPECIES *caprea* (*kap*-ree-uh), *discolor* (*dis*-kol-or), *gracilistyla*
(grax-il-iss-*tye*-luh)
ZONE 5

Few small properties today offer space to waste on the Pussy Willow, but for larger properties it is fun to have one plant or so, even if the early flowering shoots must only be enjoyed indoors. The Willows listed here are native to the United States and Asia.

USES  For early spring flower arrangements. Shoots can be cut in winter, brought indoors and forced into bloom. Bushes are not especially decorative in themselves, but they fit naturally into semi-woodland or naturalized areas. They are tolerant of damp soil.

HABIT OF GROWTH  Upright, with many branches, often becoming treelike.

FLOWERS  Soft, gray catkins before the leaves, sometimes with pink or gold coloring, the male catkins being showier because of their prominent stamens.

FOLIAGE  Rather coarse, toothed leaves, grayish underneath.

ASSETS  The early, furry catkins—an assurance that spring will come.

FAULTS  Coarse shrubs not suitable for small gardens. Foliage usually becomes riddled from insect attacks.

CULTURE  Hardy and easy in average or wet soil in full sun or light shade. Cut back every few years to keep plants low.

SPECIES  *Salix caprea.* Goat Willow. Native to Europe and Asia. Called "French" Pussy Willow in many nursery catalogues. Its catkins are large, pink tinted.
*S. discolor.* The native "Pussy Willow," found in swampy areas from Nova Scotia to Virginia and Missouri. Its gray catkins are smaller than those of the preceding species, but it is nonetheless cheering when picked on a cold bleak day.
*S. gracilistyla.* From Japan and Korea. Showy catkins in rose and gold.

# RHODODENDRON

TYPE Broad-leaved evergreen
FAMILY *Ericaceae* (Ehr-ik-*ay*-see-ee)
GENUS *Rhododendron* (Roh-doh-*den*-dron)
SPECIES *carolinianum* (ka-rol-in-ee-*ay*-num), *catawbiense* (kat-aw-bee-*en*-see), *fortunei* (for-*tew*-nee-eye), *maximum* (*max*-im-mum), *racemosum* (ras-em-*moh*-sum), *Smirnowi* (*Smir*-no-wye)
ZONE See under descriptions of species, below

If the Rhododendron were as tolerant of varying climates and soils as the Rose, it might well challenge the undisputed position of first love that the Rose holds in gardeners' hearts. The Rhododendron genus is as large as it is varied (it includes the Azalea, which possesses enough differing characteristics to be handled separately on page 18). While the majority of species are native to mountainous parts of India, Burma, Tibet, and China, there are, surprisingly enough, many tropical species found in Malaya, the East Indies, New Guinea, and the Philippines. The Alpenrose, a dwarf Rhododendron, is familiar to tourists who visit the Alps, and the Carolina Rhododendron and great Rosebay are among beloved natives of parts of the eastern United States. Rhododendron species, of which only a handful are listed here, many of them outstanding in their own right and worth a place in the home garden, are especially important because of the hybrids and named selections that have been produced from them.

USES They are the supreme landscaping shrub. There are types suitable for foundation planting, for background, mid-section and foreground in shrub borders, underplantings under specimen trees such as Dogwood. They are ideal for the edges of woodland and can, in fact, be continued throughout wooded areas, where they thrive in high, cool shade from Oaks, Pines, Birches. (While not many new homeowners today inherit established woodland as a part of their new property, it is perfectly feasible to plant a woodland, even though pocket-sized, which will quickly make a hospitable environment and setting for Rhododendrons.) There are many dwarf Rhododendrons suitable for rock gardens, rock walls. Rhododendrons can make a formal garden more formal, an informal setting more delightful.

HABIT OF GROWTH Spreading and rounded, to about 6 feet, but many Rhododendrons become treelike, eventually reaching 20–40 feet, depending on type and climate. Others can remain low, reaching only 3 feet or less in twenty years. Some form thickets, rooting each time a branch remains in contact with the soil.

FLOWERS  Colors range from red, lavender, and purple to salmon, pink, rose, yellow, and white. They are usually carried in a truss, each flower bell-shaped or broadly funnel-shaped, with stamens prominent. Some are fragrant. The flowering period of Rhododendrons is essentially spring, but it can be extended at both ends of this season by planting a full range of Rhododendrons, both species and hybrids.

FOLIAGE  Handsome, leathery, evergreen leaves, often glossy and smooth above. There is often a rusty-colored or buff, felt-like covering on the undersides, which sometimes extends to bark and flower buds. The actual green coloring of leaves ranges from bright green to greens with gray, maroon, blue, or purple undertones. The alternate leaves vary greatly in size and shape, depending on the species or variety.

ASSETS  Unparalleled as a landscaping shrub, attractive for every season, in or out of bloom. The Rhododendron is long lived, easy to transplant and requires a minimum of care. The entire genus is fascinating to gardener, collector, hybridizer, and nurseryman.

FAULTS  Rhododendrons must have acid, humusy soil, a need which restricts their growing to those who garden in regions where the soil is naturally acid or can be made so. They prefer a moist atmosphere, with light shade, and only a few very hardy types thrive in the severe, dry cold of the inland United States, or under the extreme conditions of the deep South.

CULTURE  Soil and fertilizer requirements for the Rhododendron are generally the same as for the Azalea (they are given on page 20). The soil must be acid, well-drained but able to retain moisture. An ideal soil mixture is about half soil and half humus, in the form of peat moss and/or leafmold. Rhododendrons can stand more shade than Azaleas, but their foliage is less tolerant of drying, winter winds. They should therefore be set out where they receive some protection from wind and sun in the winter as well as very hot weather in the summer. In common with Azaleas, the soil surface around Rhododendrons should be in a constant mulch—leafmold derived from decomposed Oak leaves is ideal. In fact, it is a good practice to maintain a constant pile of leaves which, as they decompose, can be spread around Rhododendrons. It is essential that Rhododendrons receive ample water after planting as well as during periods of drought.

PROPAGATION  The same as for Azaleas except the amateur without the facilities of a greenhouse had better forego trying to root cuttings of Rhododendrons. This is a specialized technique and is described in books devoted exclusively to Rhododendrons. Home gardeners can raise Rhododendrons from seed very readily and can also be successful at layering and air-layering branches.

PESTS AND DISEASES  *Chlorosis,* present when leaves are pale green or yellow with veins outlined in bright green, can usually be corrected by the use of iron chelates (Sequestrene). *Lace Wing Fly,* most troublesome when Rhododendrons are growing in sunny, dry situations, can be recognized by uneven, lighter or white stippling of the leaves, caused by the sucking of the flies underneath. It is a stubborn pest and moving the plant into a shadier spot is recommended over trying to control it with a spray such as nicotine sulphate, lindane, or malathion. *Black Vine Weevil* or *Taxus Weevil* is a snout beetle which is proving to be a serious pest anywhere that Rhododendrons are grown. The adult weevil feeds on the foliage at night, slicing away semicircular portions of the leaves. The grubs of the weevils are the most destructive, though, as they live in the soil around the roots, feeding on them, and sometimes the bark at the crown of the plant. Weevil grubs can damage a plant to such a degree that it eventually dies. Fair control of the grubs is obtained by sprinkling 5 per cent chlordane dust over the soil surface surrounding Rhododendron plants, at the rate of 1 lb. to 200 square feet, in the spring. As a precaution against the weevils, when transplanting or setting out new Rhododendron plants, mix a tablespoonful of 5 per cent chlordane into the soil at the bottom of the planting hole.

SPECIES AND VARIETIES There are hundreds of Rhododendron species, hybrids and named selections, only a few of which can be listed here. Gardeners in the moist, cool regions of the Pacific Northwest can grow most Rhododendrons with ease. Elsewhere, as in the Northeast, the upper South, parts of the Great Lakes region, the selection of Rhododendrons that will thrive narrows but there are still many, many good ones to choose. (Gardeners can join the American Rhododendron Society, 3514 N. Russet St., Portland 17, Oregon, for $5.00 a year. The Society has chapters in all the Rhododendron and Azalea-growing areas of the United States.) For descriptions and data concerning Rhododendron plants, consult also the catalogues of specialists listed at the end of this book.

*Rhododendron carolinianum.* Carolina Rhododendron. Beloved native of North and South Carolina and Tennessee, hardy to Zone 5 where temperatures don't fall below 10 degrees below zero. Neat, appealing habit with leaves only about 3 inches long or less, flowers—white, pink or rose—appearing in mid-May. A beautiful species, useful around homes, even in foundation plantings. Among modern hybrids with Carolina blood are P.J.M. Hybrids, introduced by Weston Nurseries, Hopkinton, Massachusetts, WINDBEAM, RAMAPO, and CONEWAGO. All are as hardy as the parent, and well suited to all landscaping purposes.

*R. catawbiense.* Catawba Rhododendron. Native from Virginia to Georgia, hardy to Zone 5. Lavender flowers in late May to early June. Height about 6 feet; its beautiful leaves, 5 inches long. ALBUM is white. An important parent of many hybrids including ROSEUM ELEGANS, KETTLEDRUM, LADY ARMSTRONG, EVER-ESTIANUM.

*R. fortunei.* Fortune Rhododendron. Species from eastern China, with fragrant, white to blush-pink flowers in late May and handsome leaves 8 inches long. Hardy in most parts of Zone 6. Important parent of many hybrids including the Dexter Hybrids originated on Cape Cod (SCINTILLATION, SKYGLOW); also of the hybrids DUKE OF YORK, DAVID GABLE, etc.

*R. maximum.* Rosebay Rhododendron. Native to eastern North America. Very hardy and large, eventually reaching 12 feet or more. (Zone 4.) Useful as hedge and screen. Hybrids include CUNNINGHAM'S WHITE, ALBUM ELEGANS, white, and many others.

*R. racemosum.* Mayflower Rhododendron. This species and the preceding giant from western China are good examples of the extremes that exist in this genus. *R. racemosum* is a small-leaved, small-flowered plant which grows slowly and may not exceed 2–3 feet. Its charming pink flowers appear early in May. It is a parent of WINDBEAM and CONEMAUGH, and a gem for the rock garden or for massing in front of taller growing shrubs.

*R. Smirnowi.* Smirnow Rhododendron. Species from the Caucasus, although not widely available from nurseries, is hardy to Zone 5, and should be better known to American gardeners. Its habit is excellent, dense and spreading, and the many flowers, in white to red, are carried in abundant clusters, usually appearing in late May. It should produce many fine hybrids.

# ROCK-ROSE

TYPE Evergreen
FAMILY *Cistaceae* (Siss-*tay*-see-ee)
GENUS *Cistus* (*Siss*-tus)
SPECIES *corbariensis* (kor-bay-ree-*en*-siss), *ladaniferus* (lad-an-*if*-er-us), *purpureus* (pur-*pew*-ree-us)
ZONE 8

Happy in drought, poor soil and blazing sun, the Rock-rose is a most useful plant for mild climates comparable to those of the Mediterranean region where it is native. In the same family and somewhat similar is Sun-rose, which is hardier.

USES   Rock-roses love hot, dry banks and slopes or any stretches of rocky terrain or sandy soil, whether it be desert or seashore, where they endure salt-laden winds. They are popular ground-cover plants in southern California.

HABIT OF GROWTH   Spreading growth to 3 or 4 feet, height the same or up to 6 feet.

FLOWERS   Crinkly textured flowers like those of a single Rose, varying in diameter from 2 to 3 inches. They last barely a day, but there are always plenty of buds to take the place of the fading flowers. Colors are white, pink, or purple, marked by yellow or maroon blotches at the base of the petals. Blooming time is summer.

FOLIAGE   Evergreen, opposite leaves, usually gray-green and aromatic, making an attractive background for the flowers.

ASSETS   Profuse bloom over a long period, plus the plant's endurance of poor soil and drought, make this an ideal selection for areas where it is hardy.

FAULTS   Difficult to transplant. Only suitable for mild climates.

CULTURE   Rock-rose likes an alkaline soil, needs perfect drainage, and thrives in rocky or sandy situations in full, baking sun. Young potted plants are easiest to establish.

PRUNING   Leggy plants can be rejuvenated by cutting back a few shoots to the base. Never cut back the entire plant at once. Constant pinching of the ends of the shoots helps keep plants compact.

SPECIES AND VARIETIES   *Cistus corbariensis.* White Rock-rose. Hybrid with dull-green leaves and white flowers. DORIS HIBBERSON has pink flowers.

*C. ladaniferus maculatus.* Brown-eyed Rock-rose. White flowers with crimson spot at base of petals. Height 3–5 feet. Blooms in June and July.

*C. purpureus.* Orchid Rock-rose. Rose-purple flowers with yellow base and maroon spots. A hybrid, and very attractive.

# *ROSE*

TYPE Deciduous
FAMILY *Rosaceae* (Roz-*ay*-see-ee)
GENUS *Rosa* (*Roh*-zah)
SPECIES *centifolia* (sen-tif-*foh*-lee-uh), *damascena* (dam-ass-*see*-nuh), *eglanteria* (egg-lan-*teer*-ee-uh), *foetida* (*fet*-id-duh), *Hugonis* (Hew-*go*-niss), *moschata* (mos-*kay*-tuh), *Moyesi* (Moh-*yes*-eye), *multiflora* (mull-tif-*floh*-ruh), *Roxburghi* (*Rox*-burg-eye), *rugosa* (roo-*goh*-suh), *spinosissima* (spye-noh-*siss*-im-uh)
ZONE See descriptions of species and varieties, below

Everyone is familiar with the modern Rose in its Hybrid Tea and Floribunda classes. Less familiar are the many Shrub Roses, some of which are hybrids and varieties of recent origin but others of which are species, looking today just as they did hundreds of years ago. Only a few of these so-called "old Roses" can be listed here. Consult catalogues of specialists for more details.

USES   As hedges; in borders where they can be combined with other shrubs, or in borders restricted to different kinds of Roses; on slopes and banks; against walls or fences; and a few, like *Rosa Hugonis,* Father Hugo's Rose, as specimens. Some can be naturalized at the edges of woodlands or other naturalistic areas. Many have flowers as valuable for cutting as those of the Hybrid Tea Rose. Rose-hip jelly can be made from the fruits.

HABIT OF GROWTH Generally large, bushy and thorny plants with graceful, arching branches, although some are stiff and will spread by suckers to form thickets. Heights vary from a few feet to 10 or 12.

FLOWERS   Single or double flowers, often very fragrant, from yellow and white to the pink, rose, and red colors found in the modern Rose. Some are variegated, the flowers being striped or blotched as in the YORK AND LANCASTER ROSE variety of *R. damascena.* Some, such as the Moss Roses (varieties of *R. centifolia*), have a green "mossy" coating on the flower buds. The Burr Rose (*R. Roxburghi*) has unusual buds that look like burrs.

FOLIAGE   Leaflets vary according to the species. Some are large and crinkly, as those of *R. rugosa;* others are refined and Fernlike, as those of Father Hugo's Rose. The Sweetbrier Rose (*R. eglanteria*) is famous for its fragrant foliage. All shrub roses are tough and resistant to diseases and insects when compared to the modern Rose.

ASSETS Tremendous hardiness, tolerance to drought, wind, even poor soil and salt spray (as in the case of *R. rugosa*), low maintenance (meaning little pruning and no dusting or spraying). Some have very fragrant flowers. The hips that follow the flowers are showy and are relished by birds.

FAULTS Many are large and spreading and may become too rampant for the average small property today.

CULTURE Grow in average, well-drained soil in full sun or very light shade. All of the coddling required by Hybrid Teas, Floribundas and climbers may be eliminated, as Shrub Roses require little if any pruning, no fertilizing. Prune in early spring to remove dead wood, if any, and to train or shape plants. Old canes can be removed at base to force new growth. In large plantings and where the plants have been set out in colonies in semi-naturalistic areas, pruning is almost impossible and can be forgotten.

SPECIES AND VARIETIES *Rosa centifolia.* Cabbage Rose. Hardy to Zone 5. Height about 6 feet. Old Rose from the Caucasus, long famous. Many, many varieties, a few of which are: ADELINE, vivid rose; RED PROVENCE, crimson and very fragrant; many Moss varieties including SALET, rosy pink; WILLIAM LOBB, crimson.
*R. damascena.* Damask Rose. From Asia Minor. Another famous old Rose with a history. Hardy to Zone 5. Height about 6 feet. Many varieties, including YORK AND LANCASTER.
*R. eglanteria.* Sweetbrier; Eglantine Rose. From Europe. Hardy to Zone 5. Height about 6 feet. Its small white flowers aren't much, but its apple-scented foliage is unique. Use this Rose as a semi-formal hedge and clip in early spring.
*R. foetida.* Austrian Brier. From Asia. Hardy to Zone 5. Height 9 feet. Flowers in beautiful colors. Varieties include AUSTRIAN COPPER, with flame petals, gold underneath, and SOLEIL D'OR, very large double orange flowers, shaded nasturtium red.
*R. Hugonis.* Father Hugo's Rose. Native to China. Hardy to Zone 6. Height 7 feet. Lovely, graceful shrub with delicate foliage, very early single yellow flower sprays.
*R. moschata.* Musk Rose. Hardy to Zone 6. Variety NASTARANA, Persian Musk Rose, considered superior to the species. It has semi-double, fragrant flowers of white tinged with pink. Modern

Musk Rose hybrids include BELINDA, bright pink flowers in pyramidal clusters, height about 6 feet; WILL SCARLET, bright red flowers.

*R. moyesi*. From western China. Hardy to Zone 6. Unusual and handsome single flowers, blood-red with bright gold centers, in mid-June.

*R. multiflora*. Widely advertised as the "living fence." Suitable for large-scale hedge plantings on vast properties, but too rampant for the small place. It will grow to 10 feet or more in height and the same in width. Zone 6.

*R. Roxburghi*. Roxburgh Rose; Burr Rose. From China and Japan. Hardy to Zone 5. Height 7 feet. Single pink flowers preceded by unusual buds. Distinctive with its peeling bark; effective in winter when seen against evergreens.

*R. rugosa*. Rugosa Rose. From the Orient. Escaped in many areas of the United States. Rugged, very hardy Rose (Zone 3), useful in seaside gardens. Can be grown in hedge and kept clipped. Many modern hybrids available include MAX GRAF, a ground cover; FLAMINGO, pink single flowers, height 5 feet; FRAU DAGMAR HARTOPP, silvery-pink flowers, height 2 feet; GROOTENDORST, fringed, cherry-red flowers, height 5 feet.

*R. spinosissima*. Scotch Rose. From Europe. Hardy to Zone 5. Height about 3 feet. Many varieties. HARISON'S YELLOW is popular, standard hybrid.

# ROSE-ACACIA

TYPE Deciduous
FAMILY *Leguminosae* (Leg-yew-min-*noh*-see)
GENUS *Robinia* (Roh-*bin*-ee-uh)
SPECIES *hispida* (*hiss*-pid-uh)
ZONE 6

Neither a Rose nor an Acacia, this native shrub of the Pea family is very pretty in bloom but is too spreading for the average suburban property. It is found in the southeastern United States.

USES Ideal for naturalizing on rural, seashore or extensive properties or elsewhere where a tall-growing, fast-spreading ground cover is needed. It can quickly cover banks and slopes and form colonies along driveways and roads. For more formal situations, standard (single-stem) specimens can make interesting accents.

HABIT OF GROWTH A suckering shrub, 3 to 6 feet high, its branches covered with red bristles. A few nurseries offer single-stemmed (standard) plants which have been grafted on another species to make small trees.

FLOWERS Very attractive Sweet Pea-like flowers, deep rose, in hanging clusters about 3 inches long, in late spring to early summer.

FOLIAGE Oval, alternate leaflets, seven to thirteen, about an inch long.

ASSETS Valuable for poor, sandy soil, where it forms interesting thickets with showy flowers, good foliage. In winter the bristly stems are colorful.

FAULTS Its invasive habit, which eliminates it from small properties.

CULTURE Grow in full sun, in well-drained soil which can be lean and sandy. Rose-acacia should only be planted where it can be left alone, so pruning is unnecessary. For those who want to experiment with it in situations where it cannot be left to spread, occasional thinning by cutting off stems and excess suckers at ground level can be practiced.

# ROSE OF SHARON

TYPE Deciduous
FAMILY *Malvaceae* (Mal-*vay*-see-ee)
GENUS *Hibiscus* (Hye-*bisk*-us)
SPECIES *syriacus* (sihr-*rye*-ak-us)
ZONE 6

Known also as Shrub Althea, the Rose of Sharon most resembles a bush bearing Hollyhock blossoms. It is native to eastern Asia and was first brought to this country in Colonial times from England, where it is known as the Syrian-rose.

USES  Rose of Sharon should be planted where its flowers, which appear from midsummer to fall, can be appreciated, for they are its only claim to glory. It can be effective as a background or occasional accent to a flower garden and can be combined with other shrubs in a mixed border. Where space is no problem, a planting of different varieties of this shrub can make an informal hedge. It is a pliable shrub and can be pruned to form a small tree, an espalier against a wall or fence, or a potted specimen in a large tub for terrace decoration.

HABIT OF GROWTH  Young plants are erect and rather stiff, but older plants become bushy and possess some grace. Ultimate height is 10 to 12 feet for most varieties.

FLOWERS  Typical Mallow flowers, saucer-shaped, with a diameter of from 4 to 5 inches. Some varieties have double flowers, but the single forms possess much more style. The blooms of some varieties are exceptionally decorative; others so-so. Both single and double flowers are illustrated here.

FOLIAGE  The leaves, three-lobed or toothed, are not distinctive. A few kinds have variegated leaves.

ASSETS  The showy flowers, which appear in summer. A second consideration is that Rose of Sharon plants are fast growing and can usually be expected to flower the first season after being set out, a characteristic valuable for beginners and those landscaping a new property.

FAULTS  The Rose of Sharon has been overplanted in many American gardens. To be considered is the Japanese beetle's appetite for both blossoms and foliage.

CULTURE   Grow in full sun in average soil which has been enriched with peat moss, rotted manure, compost or whatever humusy material is at hand. During periods of drought, leaves will wilt if the soil dries out. While mature plants are hardy enough to endure 5 to 10 degrees below zero for short periods, it is best to set out plants in spring, as newly transplanted plants do not possess the hardiness of older ones.

PRUNING   Flowers appear on growth of the current season, so any cutting back necessary to train the plants in tree or espalier form can be done in early spring. The plants do not actually require pruning, but larger flowers are produced when the branches are shortened in spring to leave four to six buds on each.

PESTS AND DISEASES   *Aphids* sometimes cluster at the tips of branches. Spray or dust with any all-purpose material that contains lindane or malathion. *Japanese beetles* can virtually ruin the flowers. Spray or dust with DDT, methoxychlor, or Sevin as beetles appear, but all these materials are deadly poisons and should be used with discretion.

VARIETIES   BLUE BIRD   (Plant Patent No. 1739) is a modern Rose of Sharon well worth growing. The introducer recommends cutting the plant back nearly to the ground each spring to keep its height within 3 or 4 feet, making it a most acceptable, compact plant for the front of a shrub border or for use as an accent in a flower garden. Each flower is about 5 inches across and is a lovely, clear lavender-blue shade. HAMABO has white flowers with a pronounced "bleeding" red eye, making an effective floral effect. JEANNE D'ARC has double white flowers. WOODBRIDGE has bright pink flowers, freely produced, while WILLIAM R. SMITH has pure white flowers.

# ST. JOHNSWORT

TYPE Semi-evergreen and deciduous
FAMILY *Hypericaceae* (Hye-pehr-ik-*kay*-see-ee)
GENUS *Hypericum* (Hye-*pehr*-ik-um)
SPECIES *calycinum* (kal-*liss*-in-um), *kalmianum* (kal-mee-*ay*-num), *moserianum* (moh-zer-ee-*ay*-num), *patulum* (*pat*-yew-lum)
ZONE See descriptions of species, below

These are eye-catching small shrubs in late spring and summer when their waxy, sunny flowers appear. There are many kinds of St. Johnswort, some of which are herbaceous and suited to the flower and rock garden. The St. Johnsworts listed here are truly woody. They are virtually world citizens, with species scattered over North America, Europe and Asia.

**USES** In foreground groupings of shrub borders, in foundation plantings or as low flowering hedges along walks, drives, walls or fences, and as ground cover on sunny slopes and banks.

**HABIT OF GROWTH** Bushy and mounded, or low and spreading, with heights ranging from 1 foot to 5 feet, depending on the species and climate.

**FLOWERS** Bright yellow, cup-shaped flowers with prominent stamens, of a waxy texture, and rather fragrant. They vary from 2 to 3 inches across and are produced singly or in few-flowered clusters. Flowers may appear in late spring or early summer and are usually produced well into the fall.

**FOLIAGE** Heart-shaped leaves, generally about 2 to 2½ inches long, bright green or blue-green, and evergreen or semi-evergreen in mild climates, deciduous in cold climates.

**ASSETS** The showy, golden flowers in summer that smother the plants, and tolerance for dry, sandy soil and sunny situations.

**FAULTS** The flowers appeal to Japanese beetles. Some plants can become scraggly unless kept compact by early spring pruning. Not all Hypericums are rock hardy, but fortunately there are kinds for all climates.

**CULTURE** Easy in well-drained, even sandy, soil in full sun. Increase by dividing in early spring, or by severing stems that have layered.

**PRUNING** Flowers appear on current season's growth, so prune in early spring. Even when top growth of the taller St. Johnsworts has not been winterkilled to any degree, it is best to shorten the stems or even to remove them at the ground surface to keep the plants bushy.

SPECIES AND VARIETIES  *Hypericum calycinum.* Aaronsbeard St. Johnswort. Native to Europe, Asia Minor. Bright yellow flowers, 3 inches across, beginning in July. Height, about 1 foot. Spreads rapidly by stolons; ideal ground cover for sandy soil. Tolerates light shade. Hardy to zero. Zone 6.

*H. kalmianum.* Native from Quebec to Illinois and very hardy. Bright golden flowers in summer. Height about 3 feet. Zone 5.

*H. moserianum.* Hybrid between *H. patulum* and *H. calycinum.* Called "Goldflower." Yellow flowers in July on spreading, foot-tall plants. Long-blooming ground cover. Hardy to 5 and 10 degrees (Zone 7); useful on West Coast.

*H. patulum.* Native to Japan. Height about 3 feet. Varieties include HENRYI, yellow flowers in July, height about 3 feet (Zone 7); HIDCOTE, golden cups from late June on, height from 18 inches to 4 feet or so (Zone 6); SUNGOLD, free-flowering variety with bright yellow flowers all summer, height about 2 feet. Zone 5.

## *SAND-MYRTLE*

TYPE Evergreen
FAMILY *Ericaceae* (Ehr-ik-*ay*-see-ee)
GENUS *Leiophyllum* (Lye-oh-*fill*-um)
SPECIES *buxifolium* (bux-if-*foh*-lee-um)
ZONE 6

This acid-soil lover is a pet of collectors who specialize in the Heath family. It is charming but of limited usefulness compared to other general-purpose shrubs. It is native to sandy soils from New Jersey to Florida.

USES   Ideal in rock gardens or as ground cover, especially in front of Rhododendrons, Azaleas, and other acid-soil plants. It is also of good scale for mixing into gardens of Heath (*Erica*) and Heather (*Calluna*), as similar soils and exposures suit all these plants.

HABIT OF GROWTH   Low-growing, compact, to 18 inches or so.

FLOWERS   White flowers, about ¼ inch across, in packed clusters at the ends of branches in May.

FOLIAGE   Attractive, small shiny green leaves, oval, somewhat like those of Box; usually alternate.

ASSETS   Pretty, small shrubs, of value in acid-soil regions and considered choice by conservationists and wildflower collectors. They will grow in sandy, peaty soil.

FAULTS   Sand-myrtle needs acid soil, is not showy enough for general use.

CULTURE   Soil must be full of peat, acid in reaction. Sand-myrtle will grow in sun or light shade.

# *SAPPHIREBERRY*

TYPE Deciduous
FAMILY *Symplocaceae* (Sim-ploh-*kay*-see-ee)
GENUS *Symplocos* (Sim-*ploh*-kos)
SPECIES *paniculata* (pan-ik-yew-*lay*-tuh)
ZONE 6

Sapphireberry is special for its jewel-like, bright blue berries, a fall treat for the color-sensitive gardener. It is a native of the Himalayan region of Japan and China, and is also called Asiatic Sweetleaf.

USES   As background for a mixed border of shrubs, as accent in a perennial garden, or as specimen shrubs in a lawn area or near a terrace where a neat shrub of treelike form is needed.

HABIT OF GROWTH   Somewhat reminiscent of the Hawthorn as to form, foliage, and flowers, the Sapphireberry grows like a small tree, slowly reaching 10 to 15 feet.

FLOWERS   While the berries are the outstanding characteristic of this shrub, its flowers are a dividend, too. They are borne in profuse panicles in spring and are white and fragrant. The beautiful blue berries appear in the fall and are as appealing to birds as to gardeners.

FOLIAGE   Attractive, alternate, finely toothed leaves.

ASSETS   A neat and elegant shrub, hardy and easy to grow. Once seen, the beauty of its berries is unforgettable and for this reason alone it should be on the "must" list of any shrub collector.

FAULTS   The fleeting effect of its fruit display is a defect for those who want to look at the same thing for a long period. Yet worse is the fact that this shrub is hard to find in most American nurseries.

CULTURE   The Sapphireberry grows well in sun or light shade, in average soil, and is free from pests and diseases. It is easy to transplant and requires no special pruning. It can be propagated by planting the berries, which usually don't germinate until the second year.

# SARGENT'S CRAB-APPLE

TYPE Deciduous
FAMILY *Rosaceae* (Roz-*ay*-see-ee)
GENUS *Malus* (*May*-lus)
SPECIES *Sargenti* (Sar-*jent*-eye)
ZONE 5

234 FAVORITE FLOWERING SHRUBS

Most Flowering Crab-apples, beautiful though they are, soon make large spreading trees, often outgrowing the space allotted them. Not so the Sargent's Crab-apple, a neat, low-growing species from Japan, well suited to contemporary, space-restricted gardens and homes. (The Midget, Kaido, or Fragrant Crab, *M. micromalus,* grows about 12 feet high but keeps a pyramidal shape, spreading only about 4 feet. One nursery, Wayside Gardens, offers named varieties of a few choice Crabs grafted onto very dwarf understock, thereby making the plants suitable for shrub borders, etc.)

USES   As a lawn specimen. The fruits are liked by birds.

HABIT OF GROWTH   Treelike habit to 6 feet; spreads eventually to 10 to 12 feet.

FLOWERS   Single white, fragrant flowers with gold stamens, in mid-May. The apples that follow are dark red, long-lasting, ¼ inch across, and dangle on long stems.

FOLIAGE   The leaves turn orange-to-red in the fall.

ASSETS   A neat, attractive habit, pleasant flowers, and fruit.

FAULTS   When planting, the eventual spread must be considered.

CULTURE   Hardy and easy to grow in full sun, average, well-drained soil. Allow it to take a natural, mounded form, pruning only as necessary to remove crossing branches.

# SHADBLOW

TYPE Deciduous
FAMILY *Rosaceae* (Roz-*ay*-see-ee)
GENUS *Amelanchier* (Am-el-*lank*-ee-ur)
SPECIES *grandiflora* (gran-dif-*floh*-ruh)
ZONE 4

Shadblow, also called Serviceberry, is responsible for the short-lived but lovely filmy patches of white scattered through open woodlands in spring over much of this country. The white flowers show up well, as they appear before their own leaves, as well as those of other trees, have opened. Their beauty is fleeting compared to the long-lasting display made by the white flowers of Dogwood. There are several Amelanchier species, most of which flower when young and which make shrublike growth, but these are not included here because eventually they become treelike. *Amelanchier grandiflora* is of hybrid origin, its parents being *A. canadensis* and *A. laevis*. Other common names applied to all the Shadblows are Juneberry, Bilberry, Canadian Medlar, and—by the English—Snowy Mespilus.

USES   The Shadblows are best in informal and naturalistic settings. They make good companion backgrounds for spring bulbs (the Dutch have planted them throughout the Keukenhof woodland gardens), for evergreen plants such as Rhododendron, Mountain-laurel, Pine, Hemlock. They certainly belong in light woodland areas taken over for gardening and should be added to arboretums, large or small, private or public, as an example of a choice and beloved native plant. Branches can be cut in early winter and forced into flower indoors.

HABIT OF GROWTH   Bushy growth which may become tree-like, to 10 feet or more, with horizontal branching. Plants are more shrubby and compact in full sun, thin and irregular in a woodland. Mature bark is gray and mottled and can be attractive.

FLOWERS   White, five-petaled flowers in racemes, 2 inches or more long, at the ends of twigs and along the branches, in mid-April to early May. *A. grandiflora* has the largest flowers of any, and there is also a rose-colored form. The flowers are followed by edible fruit, mostly consumed by birds.

FOLIAGE   Alternate, toothed leaves, after the flowers, with a purple cast at first. Foliage takes on yellow and orange coloring in fall.

ASSETS   Graceful and desirable for its ethereal, early-spring flower display in woodlands and naturalistic plantings.

FAULTS   Of no value whatsoever for a small property where every plant must count. Also, the flowers do not last long.

CULTURE   Easy in average, well-drained soil containing peat moss and/or leafmold. *A. grandiflora* is usually grafted, so shoots coming from the understock must be cut off if the flowering character of this species is to be retained.

# *SKIMMIA*

TYPE Evergreen
FAMILY *Rutaceae* (Roo-*tay*-see-ee)
GENUS *Skimmia* (*Skim*-mee-uh)
SPECIES *japonica* (jap-*pon*-ik-uh)
ZONE 7

A nigh-perfect little evergreen of interest to collectors in the North, where it is not completely hardy. It is native to Japan.

USES   In foundation plantings; in foreground of mixed shrub plantings, especially of Rhododendrons and other broad-leaved evergreens; in tubs.

HABIT OF GROWTH   Slow-growing, rounded or moundlike, eventually to 4 feet.

FLOWERS   One-sexed, yellow-white flowers, small, fragrant, in short panicles at the ends of branches, in late April or early May. Flowers on the male plants are slightly larger, more fragrant. Bright red berries follow bloom on the female plants and are showy in the fall. There is a white-berried form. A male and a female plant must be grown near each other to obtain fruit.

FOLIAGE   Evergreen, alternate leaves, leathery and fleshy, about 4 to 5 inches long and yellow-green in color. In full sun, leaves are almost yellow or "washed-out."

ASSETS   The fragrant flowers, showy fruit, neat, slow-growing habit, and year-round attractive leaves. It is also shade-tolerant.

FAULTS   Plants need shade when sun is brightest, or foliage will fade. Not reliably hardy in the North unless protected.

CULTURE   Grow in acid, well-drained, humusy soil such as is provided for Rhododendrons and Azaleas. Use peat moss in the soil mixture when planting. Best in shade, needing only a few hours of sun a day to form flowers. Do not prune other than to remove winterkilled parts, if any, and to remove withered berry stalks.

# SMOKE-TREE

TYPE Deciduous
FAMILY *Anacardiaceae* (An-ah-kar-dee-*ay*-see-ee)
GENUS *Cotinus* (*Kot*-in-us)
SPECIES *coggygria* (kog-*jeeg*-ree-uh)
ZONE 5

Whether called Smoke-bush or Smoke-tree—and both names are used—there's no question about the "smoke," as this shrub at a distance can appear to be enveloped in a smoky haze. It is native from southern Europe to Asia.

USES Best on large properties as a lawn specimen or as a transition shrub between tall trees and the lawn area. It can also serve in the background of a very broad shrub border.

HABIT OF GROWTH Large shrub, eventually to about 12 feet, broad and irregularly rounded in form.

FLOWERS Graceful, billowy panicles of green flowers in early June, soon turning to mauve or purple due to fruit development and remaining "smoky" throughout the summer.

FOLIAGE Purple or bluish, oval leaves which turn orange and red in the fall.

ASSETS A distinctive shrub with its plumy panicles which remain effective all summer. Foliage color, whether purple as it is in the variety *purpureus,* or orange or red of the common species in the fall, is an added attraction. A third consideration is Smoke-tree's tolerance for poor, dry soil and for city conditions.

FAULTS Once established, it is hard to transplant. It is rather large and broad for small properties and can appear too exotic unless carefully placed.

CULTURE Easy in full sun in well-drained average soil; will tolerate even dry and lean soil.

VARIETIES In addition to the common Smoke-tree there is the variety *C. coggygria purpureus,* with purple foliage all spring and summer that turns to yellow and orange in the fall. Its plumes are richly purple. NOTCUTT (Plant Patent No. 1457) is a deeper copper-purple selection.

# SNOW-WREATH

TYPE Deciduous
FAMILY *Rosaceae* (Roz-*ay*-see-ee)
GENUS *Neviusia* (Nev-ee-*yew*-see-uh)
SPECIES *alabamensis* (al-lah-bah-*men*-siss)
ZONE 6

The botanical name of this shrub is easier to remember when it is known that it was named after R. D. Nevius, who discovered it, along with W. S. Wyman, in 1857 near Tuscaloosa, Alabama. It is native to parts of the southeastern United States but is perfectly hardy in regions where temperatures may dip to 10 degrees below zero.

USES   Best in foreground plantings among other shrubs.

HABIT OF GROWTH   Graceful, rounded clumps of arching branches from 3 to 5 feet long. The plants send up numerous suckers at the base.

FLOWERS   Very pretty, rather unusual white or greenish feathery flowers, without petals but with showy stamens, in late spring. The flowers are clustered closely along the stems, making the attractive effect that gives this shrub its common name. Flowering branches should be attractive in arrangements.

FOLIAGE   Alternate leaves, 3 inches long, bright green and toothed.

ASSETS   It is hard to evaluate this shrub because it is not widely known nor available, yet it is a native American plant that has unique flowers. Probably for the collector and for the gardener who cherishes native plants.

FAULTS   Snow-wreath is rated low for all-season effect. It is rarely listed by nurseries.

CULTURE   Grow in well-drained, average soil in full sun or light shade. Easily propagated by removal of suckers.

# SPICE BUSH

TYPE Deciduous
FAMILY *Lauraceae* (Law-*ray*-see-ee)
GENUS *Lindera* (Lin-*deer*-uh)
SPECIES *benzoin* (*ben*-zoh-in)
ZONE 4

Early blooming—just before Forsythia and Cornelian-cherry— the Spice Bush can give quiet delight to an otherwise colorless landscape with its yellow flowers. The Spice Bush, sometimes listed in catalogues under its old name of *Benzoin aestivale,* is native to wetlands of the eastern half of North America. From the point of view of conservation alone—much of its native haunts give way yearly to the bulldozer—it should be considered by gardeners who have space for it.

USES Spice Bush thrives in moist, lightly shaded area. In the home garden, it has a place in shrub borders as a background plant.

HABIT OF GROWTH Vase-shaped upright shrub from 8 to 15 feet.

FLOWERS Spice Bush's fuzzy, bunched flowers appear before the leaves, opening bright yellow but gradually progressing to a chartreuse. They have a mild spicy scent. Scarlet berries appear in fall.

FOLIAGE Bright green, oval leaves in spring and summer which turn to yellow in the fall.

ASSETS Its early yellow flowers which clothe the branches before the leaves appear. Its yellow foliage in fall. Its tolerance of moist soil.

FAULTS Spice Bush is for people who enjoy spring early. Its gentle charm is easily outshone by *Azalea mucronulatum,* Forsythia, and other spring-flowering shrubs.

CULTURE Grows easily in average soil but tolerates moist soil and light shade. It has no special pruning requirements.

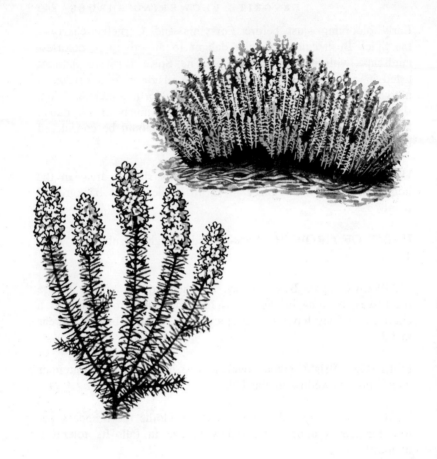

# SPIKE-HEATH

TYPE Evergreen
FAMILY *Ericaceae* (Ehr-ik-*ay*-see-ee)
GENUS *Bruckenthalia* (Brook-en-*tay*-lee-uh)
SPECIES *spiculifolia* (spik-yew-lif-*foh*-lee-uh)
ZONE 6

A very dwarf evergreen from eastern Europe and Asia Minor, to grow with Heaths, Heathers, Azaleas and Rhododendrons (which see).

USES  As ground cover, either on a sunny slope or bank; as a foreground planting for taller shrubs of the Heath family; and in rock gardens.

HABIT OF GROWTH  Moundlike growth up to 9 inches high, similar to that of Heath and Heather.

FLOWERS  Inch-long spikes of lovely pink "bells," about ⅛ inch long, making a showy, long-lasting display beginning in June. There is also a white-flowered variety, ALBA.

FOLIAGE  Glossy, deep-green, needlelike leaves in dense whorls around the stems.

ASSETS  Long-lasting, clear-pink flower spikes, pleasing evergreen foliage, and neat plant habit.

FAULTS  The Spike-heath must be grown in acid soil.

CULTURE  It needs the same soil as Heath and Heather, a sand, peaty soil, well drained, in a sunny or lightly shaded area. The Spike-heath increases its spread slowly and for this reason, as well as its low stature, at least three to six plants should be grouped together in order for it to be effective. The only pruning necessary is removal of faded flower spikes.

# SPIREA

TYPE Deciduous

FAMILY *Rosaceae* (Roz-*ay*-see-ee)

GENUS *Spiraea* (spye-*ree*-uh)

SPECIES *arguta* (ar-*gew*-tuh), *Billiardi* (*Bil*-yar-dye), *bullata* (bul-*lay*-tuh), *Bumalda* (Bu-*mal*-duh), *japonica* (jap-*pon*-ik-uh), *macrothyrsa* (mak-roh-*thir*-sah), *nipponica* (nip-pon-*ik*-uh), *prunifolia* (prew-nif-*foh*-lee-uh), *sanssouciana* (san-soo-see-*ay*-nuh), *Thunbergi* (*Thun*-ber-jye), *trilobata* (try-loh-*bah*-tuh), *Vanhouttei* (Van-*hoot*-ee-eye)

ZONE 4, 5

The Spireas vary so much in flowering form and blooming time that it is hard to believe that they all belong to the same genus. For instance, compare Bridal-wreath, with its garlands of white flower clusters in spring, to the Pink Spirea (*Spiraea macrothyrsa*), with its fluffy pink plumes in summer. And the ever-popular Anthony Waterer Spirea has flat-topped, crimson flower clusters in early summer. This genus is a large one, with many species and hybrids; the forms included here are those most readily available from nurseries.

USES   As background or foreground shrubs in a mixed border; as flowering hedges; as specimens; and as cut-flower material. (Uses for a given species depend, of course, on its form and height.)

HABIT OF GROWTH   Usually graceful, arching shrubs, although some are upright and rather stiff and others make mound-like growth, rather low in height.

FLOWERS   Clusters of white, pink, or rosy-red flowers in racemes, or along the stems, or in pyramidal spires at the ends of stems, or in flat-topped heads, again at the ends of stems. Some Spireas flower in early to late spring; others start in summer and may last to early fall.

FOLIAGE   Alternate leaves, in some blue-green, in a few turning to attractive autumn shades. Leaves are generally dense enough to give the shrubs substance when out of bloom.

ASSETS   Hardy, easy-to-grow-and-care-for shrubs with varied flowers that are long lasting and showy. They fit well into a mixed shrub border, blending well with other shrubs; their foliage is dense enough to make a good screen except in the winter months. Many are compact and low, making them useful for modern gardens.

FAULTS   Some Spireas are better than others. (However, the ones listed here are all worthwhile and available.) The Bridal-wreaths are common shrubs, yet nevertheless striking in flower.

CULTURE No special soil requirements other than well-drained soil and a sunny exposure, or one with very light shade. Spirea is easy to transplant in spring or fall.

PRUNING Not much is necessary. Occasional thinning of shoots at base will force strong new wood. Spring-flowering kinds like *S. arguta, prunifolia, Thunbergi, Vanhouttei,* etc., flower on new growth; therefore old growth can be cut down in early spring if necessary. Removal of fading flowers of summer types stimulates more flower production the same season.

SPECIES AND VARIETIES *Spiraea arguta.* Sometimes called "Foam of May." Hybrid. Moundlike form, to 5–6 feet. Racemes of white flowers clothe branches in late April, early May. Compact form available (about 3 feet). Zone 4.

*S. Billiardi.* Hybrid. Bright pink flowers in dense pyramid-shaped spikes in midsummer. Height, about 5 feet. Has suckering habit. Zone 5. Similar to the native Hardhack or Steeple-bush (*S. tomentosa*) seen in pastures and fields of eastern North America.

*S. bullata.* From Japan. Often listed in catalogues as CRISPIFOLIA. Rosy-red flower clusters cover plant in July. Moundlike growth; to 1 foot. Zone 5.

*S. Bumalda.* ANTHONY WATERER is the common form. Bright red flowers in flat clusters in late June, lasting into July. Height 2 feet. Zone 4.

*S. japonica.* Native to Japan. COCCINEA, a brighter ANTHONY WATERER, is 4 feet high. Flowers in June. Zone 5.

*S. macrothyrsa.* Hybrid. Pyramidal spikes of pink flowers with a long blooming season, starting in early summer. Height 3 to 4 feet. Zone 5.

*S. nipponica.* Native to Japan. Variety SNOWMOUND makes compact mound, with branches strung with white flower clusters in June. Height 3 to 4 feet. Zone 5.

*S. prunifolia.* This is the true Bridal-wreath. Native to China and Korea. Form available has white double flowers all along arching branches in May. Foliage takes on orange tints in fall. Height about 8 feet. Zone 5.

*S. sanssouciana.* Hybrid. Handsome, fluffy rose flowers in

pyramidal spikes 12 inches long, in midsummer. Height about 4 to 5 feet. Zone 5.

*S. Thunbergi.* Native to China and Japan. Pretty white flower clusters along branches before leaves, in late April to May. Height about 5 feet. Zone 5.

*S. trilobata.* Native to China. Named variety is SWAN LAKE, with white flower clusters in late May to June. Height 3 to 4 feet. Foliage is lobed. Zone 3.

*S. Vanhouttei.* This popular Spirea is a hybrid, one of its parents being *S. trilobata.* It, too, is often called Bridal-wreath. White flower clusters along the branches in June, a little later than *S. prunifolia.* Height 6 feet. Zone 4.

# STAR MAGNOLIA

TYPE Deciduous
FAMILY *Magnoliaceae* (Mag-nohl-ee-*ay*-see-ee)
GENUS *Magnolia* (Mag-*nohl*-ee-uh)
SPECIES *stellata* (stel-*lay*-tuh)
ZONE 5

The Star Magnolia is part of the poetry of spring. A native of Japan, it is one of the few Magnolias which can be truly classed as a shrub, although this may seem a contradiction as almost all the Magnolias have the ability to flower when very young and only a few feet tall.

USES The Star Magnolia is ideal for accent, either on a lawn or near a terrace, a pool or as a focal point in a mixed shrub border. It combines well with both broad-leaved evergreens and other deciduous plants. Wherever it is used, it should be placed so that its starry white flowers, which appear very early in the spring, can stand out—as against green grass, evergreens, or a blue sky.

HABIT OF GROWTH Star Magnolia is sometimes treelike in habit, forming a single stem, but usually it makes several stems to form a spreading, broad form with flowers and foliage appearing to ground level. It is slow growing but eventually may reach 12 feet or more.

FLOWERS The glistening white flowers, which appear before the leaves in early spring (April around New York), and for many weeks thereafter, from a distance look like many pointed stars but actually their many petals are more like short arrangements of wavy ribbons. They are scented. The bright red clusters of fruit, 2 inches long, which appear in late summer, can also be showy. Flower buds form in the fall.

FOLIAGE The leathery leaves, 5 inches long, have great character and are another reason why this shrub is so useful.

ASSETS First, its flowers, then its foliage and good looks, especially its winter silhouette when the irregular, dense branching habit can be enjoyed. The Pussy-willowlike flower buds also contribute to the winter charm of this shrub. The Star Magnolia is slow growing, yet flowers when only a few feet in height.

FAULTS The flowers are so eager to appear in spring that they can be marred by frost. Also the Star Magnolia is considered difficult to transplant, so a wise gardener places it carefully to avoid having to transplant it once it has become established.

CULTURE   The Star Magnolia does best in full sun, but is not a disappointment in light shade, where it produces almost as many flowers. It likes rich, humusy soil that will retain moisture during periods of drought. Planting should be done only in early spring (unless container-grown plants are available) and is safe while the flowers are blooming. If it should be necessary to transplant a Star Magnolia, dig carefully, trying not to sever the long, fleshy roots. Once the Star Magnolia is established, it needs only to be enjoyed, as it requires no pruning, no maintenance. One exception—if foliage becomes discolored and is covered with a sooty mildew, look for the Tulip-tree scale. Spray with a miscible oil, following manufacturer's directions, and repeat if necessary, as this is a serious pest.

VARIETIES   *Magnolia stellata* has a few varieties that are listed by up-to-date nurseries, probably all of hybrid origin. The most important is DR. MERRILL, a hybrid originated at Arnold Arboretum by Dr. Karl Sax, which is reputed to grow very fast and transplant easily. WATERLILY is described as a blush-pink, double-flowered variety which flowers a little later than *M. stellata,* thereby being less susceptible to frost injury. ROSEA is a pink-petaled variety or hybrid of great charm. ROYAL STAR has double flowers, blooms ten days later than *M. stellata.*

# STEWARTIA

TYPE Deciduous
FAMILY *Theaceae* (Tee-*ay*-see-ee)
GENUS *Stewartia* (Stew-*art*-ee-uh)
SPECIES *malacodendron* (mal-ak-od-*den*-dron), *monadelpha* (mon-ad-*delf*-uh), *ovata* (oh-*vay*-tuh), *pseudo-camellia* (sood-oh-kam-*mell*-ee-uh), *serrata* (ser-*ray*-tuh)
ZONE See descriptions of species, below

Almost a substitute for the Camellia yet lovely in its own right is the Stewartia. Its single white flowers do resemble those of a single Camellia and not by chance, as the two shrubs are in the same family and quite closely related. Stewartia has species native to the southern United States which are hardy in the North as well as species native to Asia.

USES  These large shrubs are best as important accents, either on a lawn or at the edge of a lawn and woodland. They can also be used in similar situations to those suitable for the Flowering Dogwood, and make good backgrounds for Azaleas and Rhododendrons.

HABIT OF GROWTH  In their native environment the various Stewartias become tall trees, but in gardens should remain at about 10 feet, at first making erect growth, eventually spreading and becoming almost as broad as high. A dividend of the Stewartia is the peeling or flaking bark of the stems and branches.

FLOWERS  Lovely, large white cups with golden or purple anthers, slightly fragrant, in late June or July.

FOLIAGE  Handsome, alternate leaves to about 3 inches long, deep green and changing to purple or orange tints, according to species, in the fall.

ASSETS  Beautiful flowers in early summer; also attractive foliage and the flaking bark, which is of special interest after the leaves have fallen. Everything about the Stewartia makes it desirable for the gardener who wants a superior plant.

FAULTS  These shrubs resent root disturbance, so once they are established transplanting should be avoided. Due to their eventual spread, they must be placed carefully on very small properties.

CULTURE  All the Stewartias like a good soil, slightly acid, that is well-drained but able to retain moisture in drought. Add large quantities of peat moss to the soil when planting. In the northern extremes of their zones, a protected location is to be preferred. Plant in sun or part shade. No pruning is necessary other than to shape or train, if desired.

SPECIES AND VARIETIES *Stewartia malacodendron.* Virginia Stewartia. Native from Virginia to Florida, Louisiana, and Arkansas, and occasionally found in Texas. Beautiful shrub, eventually to about 12 feet, considered too tender to risk beyond Washington, D.C., although it will stand 10 degrees above zero. White flowers in spring or early summer. Zone 7.

*S. monadelpha.* Native to Japan. Height about 10 feet. White flowers in July. Hardy to Zone 6.

*S. ovata.* Showy Stewartia. Native to Kentucky and Georgia. Large white flowers, nearly 3 inches across, in late June, sometimes continuing into August. Its foliage turns orange in the fall. Height about 10 feet. Its variety *grandiflora* has larger flowers, with showy purple stamens. This variety has purplish fall color. Both forms hardy to Zone 6.

*S. pseudo-camellia.* Japanese Stewartia. Native to Japan. Very large shrub. In winter its flaking bark is especially noticeable. White flowers, 2½ inches in diameter, in early July. Color of fall foliage is purple. Hardy to Zone 6.

*S. serrata.* Native to Japan. Flowers creamy white with red stains on outside petals, 2 inches across, in early July. Foliage toothed. Hardy to Zones 6, 7.

# STRAWBERRY-SHRUB

TYPE Deciduous
FAMILY *Calycanthaceae* (Kal-ik-kanth-*ay*-see-ee)
GENUS *Calycanthus* (Kal-ik-*kanth*-us)
SPECIES *floridus* (*flor*-id-us)
ZONE 5

For old times' sake, include the Strawberry-shrub, or Carolina Allspice, in a shrub border. This curious yet appealing shrub, native to the southeastern United States, was a feature of Colonial gardens, and to this day it is associated with memories of our grandmothers' and great-grandmothers' plantings. It is also called Sweet Shrub.

USES This shrub makes an effective background for a fragrant garden. It also combines with Viburnums, Lindera, Witch-hazels, and other deciduous shrubs used as a border or screen.

HABIT OF GROWTH A rounded, erect shrub, to 6 or 7 feet.

FLOWERS Interesting, "wispy," chocolate-colored flowers about 2 inches wide, at the ends of short branches in mid-May. While the color of the flowers is unusual in flowering shrubs, their real distinction comes from the fragrance, which can be very pervasive, at first sweetly aromatic, then fruity.

FOLIAGE Handsome leaves, opposite, bright green and hairy on the undersides. They are aromatic when crushed and, in the fall, turn bright yellow. The bark is also aromatic and in Colonial days was used as a substitute for cinnamon.

ASSETS The unique scent from the flowers makes Strawberry-shrub an essential plant for a garden planned for fragrance. This shrub also tolerates part shade and is very hardy.

FAULTS Where space is limited and interest in fragrant flowers of no importance, more distinctive shrubs are available. A caution to seekers of this shrub is that American nurseries appear to be flooded with plants lacking their main asset, fragrance. This is either due to widespread propagation of plants that originally lacked fragrance or, more likely, to propagation of a similar but low-fragrance species, *Calycanthus fertilis*. Therefore, it is wise to sniff before buying.

CULTURE Grow in sun or part shade in a rich soil containing plenty of such moisture-retentive materials as peat moss, compost, rotted manure. In poor, dry soil this shrub is disappointing and will make straggling growth. If you have an especially fragrant plant of the Strawberry-shrub and want to increase it, try cuttings in early summer—they should root readily. Other methods are dividing in early spring or late fall and inducing stems to "layer," which means pegging them down to root, then severing them from the plant.

PRUNING None needed, except the recommendation has been made that pinching off the tips of the branches in early spring will cause more flowers to appear.

# SUMMERSWEET

TYPE Deciduous
FAMILY *Clethraceae* (Kleth-*race*-see-ee)
GENUS *Clethra* (*Kleth*-ruh)
SPECIES *alnifolia* (al-nif-*foh*-lee-uh), *barbinervis* (bar-bin-*ner*-viss)
ZONE 4, 6

One of the delights of a summer evening is the perfume given off by Summersweet's flowers, whether it comes from the garden or is caught on a leisurely walk or drive along a country road. Summersweet, also called Sweet Pepperbush, is a native of the Atlantic seaboard and is usually found growing in damp, acid soil. Similar to it is the Japanese Clethra, *C. barbinervis,* described at the end of this section.

USES Excellent in a shrub border as background for other acid-soil shrubs, such as Azaleas and Rhododendrons. Attractive near artificial or natural pools or ponds.

HABIT OF GROWTH When completely happy, as in moist, peaty soil, Summersweet makes a handsome, bushy shrub of many stems clothed with foliage almost to the ground. Under less ideal conditions, it makes lanky growth. Height in moist soil may be 10 feet or more; 6 in dry.

FLOWERS Long-lasting, pert spikes of white flowers, especially fragrant, in early summer. The spikes, 4 to 6 inches long, appear in great profusion and last well when cut. The variety *rosea* has pink flower buds and pale pink flowers with prominent stamens.

FOLIAGE Handsome and shiny bright green leaves which are alternate, toothed, and somewhat like those of the Alder. In the fall the leaves may turn yellow.

ASSETS Summersweet's haunting, spicy fragrance from flowers that are attractive in themselves.

FAULTS Its fussiness as to soil, which must be acid.

CULTURE Given a soil to which peat moss has been generously added and which has been kept moist during drought, Summersweet can be expected to adapt itself to the home garden in which Azaleas and Rhododendrons will grow. Where soil conditions are not to its liking, not acid nor moist enough, it may languish, become lanky, and its foliage may become infested with red-spider mites. It will grow in light shade or sun. Plants can be dug from the wild, usually as rooted suckers or layers, and will need to be cut back before they will make attractive, bushy specimens. Most nurseries list all forms of Clethra and will supply young, bushy plants that are superior to collected material.

**SPECIES AND VARIETIES** *Clethra alnifolia.* Described above. In addition to the pink form, *rosea,* there is PINKSPIRE (U. S. Department of Agriculture, No. 190213), reputed to be even pinker. Hardy to Zone 4.

*C. barbinervis.* Japanese Clethra. Similar flowers, but earlier and not as rock hardy (Zone 6). This shrub's habit of growth is more spreading and taller, and it is just slightly less hardy than *C. alnifolia.*

# SUN-ROSE

TYPE Evergreen
FAMILY *Cistaceae* (Siss-*tay*-see-ee)
GENUS *Helianthemum* (Hee-lee-*anth*-em-um)
SPECIES *nummularium* (num-mew-*lay*-ree-um)
ZONE 6

Unpretentious yet pleasing subshrubs, the Sun-roses appeal to the serious rock gardener and plant collector. The species dealt with here is native to the Mediterranean region.

USES   For rock gardens and at the top of walls; for spots near garden steps; for ground cover in dry, sunny areas, whether flat or sloping; for the foreground of perennial borders; or as ground cover in mixed shrub borders in full sun.

HABIT OF GROWTH   Low-growing, informal mounds to 6 inches or so high, with a spread of about 15 to 18 inches.

FLOWERS   Cup-shaped, single or double flowers, 1 inch across, in loose racemes at the ends of the stems from early summer intermittently until fall. Colors include yellow, scarlet, white, salmon. Each flower lasts but a day.

FOLIAGE   Oval, pointed leaves, glossy and silvery underneath, the top leaves more slender than the lower.

ASSETS   Bright-colored, cheerful flowers for full sun, produced fairly freely over a long period, and attractive foliage. The low, spreading plants are especially effective among rock outcroppings.

FAULTS   The Sun-rose is hard to transplant, once established. The evergreen foliage will burn in winter in the North unless protected.

CULTURE   Full sun and good drainage are necessary. A neutral or slightly alkaline soil is preferred. In late summer, cut back straggling shoots that have flowered. The Sun-rose is hardy to 10 degrees below zero when covered consistently by snow; otherwise spread evergreen boughs over the plants to keep the foliage from burning and the shoots from dying back. Do not fertilize, but apply ground limestone occasionally if plants are in acid-soil region.

VARIETIES    Several named varieties are available. Good ones include FLAME, single, coral-pink flowers; GOLDILOCKS, large, single yellow flowers, silvery foliage; JOCK SCOTT, tomato red; BOULE DE FEU, double red; SNOWBELL, double, pure white.

# *SWEETSPIRE*

TYPE Deciduous
FAMILY *Saxifragaceae* (Sax-if-rag-*gay*-see-ee)
GENUS *Itea* (*It*-ee-uh)
SPECIES *virginiana* (vir-jin-ee-*ay*-nuh)
ZONE 6

Sweetspire is also known as Virginian-willow for its slender, toothed leaves and pithy stems. It is rarely listed by nurseries but can be found in the wild in swampy places from New Jersey southward. It is a special native, of value to gardeners who are interested in native plants.

**HABIT OF GROWTH** An upright, slender-stemmed shrub 3 to 6 feet tall.

**USES** For naturalizing in colonies in woodlands along paths; for grouping around informal pools, or for front-of-the-border use among other shrubs.

**FLOWERS** Fragrant, small white flowers in spiky racemes 6 inches long, at the ends of the branches in early summer (July).

**FOLIAGE** Lance-shaped, toothed leaves, alternate, becoming bright red in the fall.

**ASSETS** Hardiness as far north as Boston and in similar climates and adaptability to moist situations as well as to well-drained soils in light shade or sun, mark this as a tolerant yet vanishing native worthy of colonizing in naturalistic settings. Its fragrant flowers are an attraction for summer and its fall foliage color can be handsome.

**FAULTS** Hard to locate. Only for the specialist and conservationist and wildflower gardener.

**CULTURE** While it prefers moist soil near streams, the Sweetspire is adaptable to drier situations. It does well in light shade as well as sun. Grow in a humusy soil. Old and weak stems can be cut out in the spring.

# TAMARISK

TYPE Deciduous

FAMILY *Tamaricaceae* (Tam-ar-ik-*kay*-see-ee)

GENUS *Tamarix* (*Tam*-ur-rix)

SPECIES *hispida* (*hiss*-pud-uh), *odessana* (oh-des-*say*-nuh), *par-viflora* (par-vif-*floh*-ruh), *pentandra* (pen-*tand*-ruh)

ZONE See descriptions of species, below

Tamarisk can be a lifesaver to summer gardens, especially those located at the seashore. The feathery flowers are pretty on the shrub as well as in arrangements. The species are native to Europe and Asia.

USES  In a mixed shrub border or a corner grouping; as a background accent for a flower garden; as an informal hedge; or as a specimen. Also as an accent and screen beside a terrace. Tamarisk is especially effective among Heath (*Erica*) and Heather (*Calluna*) plants, as all three grow in similar situations, have similar foliage and flower patterns and colors. Flower arrangers should grow one plant just for cutting—both foliage and flowers are effective.

HABIT OF GROWTH  Upright, slender-branched shrubs, open and graceful in effect.

FLOWERS  Small, feathery flowers in long racemes, beginning in midsummer or earlier and lasting until early fall. Colors are pink or deep rose.

FOLIAGE  Small, Heatherlike leaves, gray-green, as delicate and feathery as the flowers.

ASSETS  Their showy, graceful flower spires in summer and, secondly, their tolerance of sandy soils and wind, even when the wind carries salt spray.

FAULTS  On a small property one or two plants are enough, as the abundant, bright-colored flowers and delicate habit may be oppressive if too many plants are seen. Once established, plants resent being moved.

CULTURE  Tamarisk grows in average as well as lean soil in full sun. At the seashore, add peat moss to the planting hole if soil is excessively sandy. Planting is best done in early spring, and it is recommended that the plants be cut back to within 6 inches or so of the ground.

PRUNING  The summer-flowering Tamarisks flower on new growth, so spring pruning is the rule: either remove stems at ground level to keep the plants compact, or cut higher, depending on effect desired. *Tamarix parviflora* is an exception—it flowers in the spring, so pruning is done after flowering. Remove a few stems at base and shorten remaining branches to keep compact habit.

SPECIES AND VARIETIES  *Tamarix hispida.* Kashgar Tamarisk. Zone 5. Pink flowers in dense racemes in late summer. Height about 4 feet.

*T. odessana.* Zone 5. Pink flowers beginning in July; blue-green foliage. Spring pruning can keep this shrub to about 6 feet.

*T. parviflora.* Small-flowered Tamarisk. Zone 5. Similar to the preceding species except for its flowering time: May. The pink flowers, scattered in short racemes all along the stems, are produced on old wood. This shrub is effective with Tulips.

*T. pentandra.* Zone 3. Very hardy. Rosy-pink flowers, beginning in July, can almost smother the slender branches; they have a gingerbread scent. Attractive foliage is blue-green. Height about 15 feet, but by cutting back almost to the ground in early spring plants can be prevented from becoming leggy at base and can be maintained at a height of about 8 feet. PINK CASCADE (Plant Patent No. 1275) is a recent introduction with pink flowers and gray-green leaves. Height about 8 feet, but spring pruning can keep it to about 5 or 6 feet. SUMMER GLOW is listed in catalogues, has rosy-pink flowers. Height about 8 feet.

# *TRAILING-ARBUTUS*

TYPE Evergreen subshrub
FAMILY *Ericaceae* (Ehr-ik-*ay*-see-ee)
GENUS *Epigaea* (Ep-ij-*ee*-uh)
SPECIES *asiatica* (ay-zee-*at*-ik-uh), *repens* (*ree*-penz)
ZONE 3

Is Trailing-arbutus a flowering shrub? This beloved North American native (*Epigaea repens* is native, *E. astiatica* comes from Japan) is truly woody, even though its flowers are minute and it hugs the ground.

USES   In wildflower gardens, as ground cover in woodland areas or in foreground of mixed shrub plantings, on banks or slopes, or for occasional use around Rhododendrons and other acid-soil-tolerant plants. Actually, the Trailing-arbutus can be tucked into a variety of situations even on small properties, because of its small size, if trouble is taken to meet its needs. Much nonsense by well-meaning writers has appeared regarding its culture and conservation. In the past it has been ruthlessly picked, but this outrage is mild compared to the destruction of whole areas carpeted by it by the bulldozers preceding building developments. And what harm is there in digging a few clumps from the wild and trying to establish them, successfully or unsuccessfully, in the home garden? Why put them on the so-called conservation lists when land developers can wipe out whole colonies to make way for new houses or roads?

HABIT OF GROWTH   Flat, creeping, patch-forming plants.

FLOWERS   Tubular or bell-shaped flowers, about ½ inch in diameter, white, flesh-pink or pink, with a distinctive, sweet perfume. They appear in April. (The name "Mayflower" is reported to have been given the plant by the Pilgrims—after their ship.)

FOLIAGE   Leathery leaves to 3 inches long. They can be disfigured by winter burn unless protected by a heavy mulch of Oak leaves or Pine needles.

ASSETS   Trailing-arbutus is one of our choice native plants—reason enough for trying to reestablish it in home gardens. The purity of its flowers and their scent, like the Lilac, stir the senses and evoke nostalgic memories.

FAULTS  The plants need acid soil, have a very fine root system and are difficult to transplant from the wild unless immediately reestablished in similar soil.

CULTURE  Well-drained, humusy soil that is acid seems to be a requirement, although very healthy patches can be found on gravelly, lean slopes in full sun. While young, pot-grown plants from nurseries are first sources of plants for the home garden, there should be no compunction about digging patches of plants that may be native in the area. Use ample amounts of leafmold and peat moss in either case, and water the plants as necessary. Maintain a mulch of leafmold and Pine needles over and around the plants.

PROPAGATION  For those who care to try, Trailing-arbutus is surprisingly easy to root from cuttings of new growth taken in late spring to early summer. Wrap stems of cuttings in sphagnum moss, insert in a flat of peat moss and sand, water thoroughly, and cover with a tent of polyethylene. Keep in light shade. The cuttings should be rooted—shown by the young threadlike roots showing through the sphagnum—in four to six weeks, and can then be planted in a peaty soil mixture. (This method was devised by Robert S. Lemmon, who received an award from the Massachusetts Horticultural Society for his contribution to conservation.)

# *TREE PEONY*

TYPE Deciduous
FAMILY *Ranunculaceae* (Rah-nun-kew-*lay*-see-ee)
GENUS *Paeonia* (Pee-*oh*-nee-uh)
SPECIES *lutea* (*lew*-tee-uh), *suffruticosa* (suf-frew-tik-*koh*-suh)
ZONE 5

The Tree Peony—not treelike at all, but named as it is because its stems and branches are woody rather than herbaceous like the common garden Peony—is in the same category as the modern Rose. It has magnificent flowers but an otherwise rather stiff and unattractive habit, the beautiful flowers seeming almost to have been pinned on the plant. Both Tree Peony species are native to China.

USES   Plants can be grouped in the foreground of mixed shrub borders, especially among Rhododendrons, or used as special accents in perennial borders. Useful also as a garden unto themselves, especially with an evergreen background which will provide protection from wind and make an effective setting for the flowers; good against walls and fences.

HABIT OF GROWTH   Bushy shrubs from 3 to 6 feet tall, with a rather angular branching habit.

FLOWERS   Very beautiful flowers in white, pink, rose, and yellow, single and double, carried at the ends of the branches. Most of the Tree Peonies offered by nurseries are hybrids and differ from the double-flowered garden Peonies in that their centers, of many yellow stamens, are more open. Tree Peony flowers are generally huge, may measure from 9 to 12 inches in diameter. Petals are usually ruffled, frilled or crinkled to some degree. Blooming time is late May.

FOLIAGE   Three to five leaflets, which are broad and lobed.

ASSETS   The beautiful, exotic flowers.

FAULTS   These shrubs offer little interest after the flowers have passed.

CULTURE   Although considered temperamental, Tree Peonies are easy to grow once properly established. They will endure winter temperatures to 10 degrees below zero, but a loose mulch should be applied over the surface of their root area after the ground has frozen in the first winter after planting. As with herbaceous Peonies, fall is planting time, and once the shrubs are established, transplanting should be avoided. Choose a sunny or slightly shaded location where there will be protection from winter winds. The soil should be well drained and rich. Add compost, well-rotted manure if available, or leafmold or peat moss to the planting hole. Occasional applications of ground limestone—if the soil is very acid—wood ashes, if available, and superphosphate are beneficial.

PRUNING Virtually none needed. On very old, long-established plants, removing weak stems at the base is occasionally practiced.

SPECIES AND VARIETIES *Paeonia lutea*. Low shrub to 3 feet, with yellow flowers about 4 inches across. The flowers often droop in such a way as to be almost hidden, but this species is important as a parent of many hybrids.

*P. suffruticosa*. Sometimes listed as *P. moutan*. Tree Peony. This shrub may reach 6 feet. Its red, rose or white flowers may measure 1 foot across. There are many, many named varieties, most of which are hybrids. All are worthwhile; consult catalogues for descriptions. (Tree Peonies may seem expensive compared to some other shrubs. Propagating and growing them to a saleable, flowering size is a slow process.)

# *VIBURNUM*

TYPE Deciduous and evergreen
FAMILY *Caprifoliaceae* (Kap-rif-foh-lee-*ay*-see-ee)
GENUS *Viburnum* (Vye-*burn*-um)
SPECIES *Bitchiuense* (Bit-chew-*en*-se), *Bodnantense* (Bod-nant-*en*-see), *Burkwoodi* (*Burk*-wood-eye), *carlcephalum* (Karl-*sef*-a-lum), *Carlesi* (*Karl*-ess-eye), *Chenaulti* (Shay-*noll*-tye), *fragrans* (*fray*-granz), *Juddi* (*Judd*-eye), *odoratissimum* (oh-dor-at-*tiss*-im-um), *opulus* (*op*-yew-lus), *tomentosum* (toh-men-*toh*-sum)
ZONE See descriptions of species, below

The Viburnums are a vast clan of many shrubs, some valued for their fall berry display, others for their spring flowers. The ones listed here have showy flowers. There are Viburnums native to North America, Europe, and Asia.

USES As specimens and accents, as background and intermediate subjects in a mixed shrub border, at the edge of woods and in naturalistic settings. Where space permits, a border or planting devoted to different kinds of Viburnums—both flowering and fruiting types—can be challenging. Birds are attracted to Viburnum berries.

HABIT OF GROWTH There is great variation. Viburnums are upright, often shrubby and dense, varying in ultimate height from about 6 feet to as high as 9 or 15 feet or higher. In the case of *V. tomentosum,* the branching and flowering arrangement is in tiers.

FLOWERS It is possible to have a Viburnum in flower from early spring to June if several species and hybrids are selected. The flowers are in rounded clusters or umbels, white or pink, some with delightful fragrance reminiscent of Trailing-arbutus. Others have balls of snowy sterile flowers (*V. tomentosum sterile,* Japanese Snowball) which are especially showy. The fruit clusters of Viburnums, which may be red, orange, yellow or black, can be reason enough for growing these shrubs.

FOLIAGE Generally attractive; in some species it is evergreen or semi-evergreen in the South and in mild climates. The leaves are opposite, deeply veined, with toothed edges. A few have lobed leaves like the Maple. Fall coloring can be effective, varying from bright red to a dark purple.

ASSETS Charming and delicate or handsome and showy flowers, beginning in early spring, and depending on the species, continuing to early June. Some Viburnums are as delightfully fragrant as any flowering shrub. Fruit clusters of most of the Viburnums that are valued for their flowers are of secondary importance. (Consult nursery catalogues for Viburnums with especially showy fruit displays.) Viburnums have attractive foliage as well as generally good growth habits. They are easy to grow and require little, if any, maintenance.

FAULTS   A few Viburnums eventually become very large shrubs so must be placed with care if they are not to outgrow their site.

CULTURE   Viburnums need well-drained yet moist soil, moderately rich, in full sun or very light shade. Add peat moss, compost and, if available, well-rotted manure, to the planting hole. The very early flowering Viburnums, like *V. fragrans* and *V. Bodnantense,* should be placed where they receive some protection for their precocious buds and flowers. Viburnums require little pruning other than occasional removal of winterkilled portions.

PESTS AND DISEASES   *Viburnum opulus* is attacked by aphids which distort foliage and tip growth. Control is by spraying with lindane or malathion before the aphids have caused the leaves to curl. Viburnums are allergic to sulphur; it causes defoliation.

SPECIES AND VARIETIES   *Viburnum Bitchiuense.* From Japan. Similar to *V. Carlesi* but slightly hardier and with smaller leaves and flower clusters. Plant habit is more open. Zone 5.
*V. Bodnantense.* Hybrid (*V. fragrans* and *V. grandiflorum*) recently introduced from England. Fragrant pink flower clusters in early spring. Probably hardy to Zone 5.
*V. Burkwoodi.* Hybrid (*V. Carlesi* and *V. utile*) with fragrant, white and pink flower clusters and semi-evergreen foliage in mild climates. It is easy to propagate (the home gardener can take cuttings in late spring) and therefore doesn't have to be grafted as does *V. Carlesi,* so is considered superior to the parent. Zone 5.
*V. carlcephalum.* Fragrant Snowball. Hybrid (*V. Carlesi* and *V. macrocephalum*) from England, introduced in the United States by Wayside Gardens. Very fragrant, rounded clusters of white flowers in May. Bright fall foliage. Hardy to Zone 5 in protected areas.
*V. Carlesi.* Very popular species from Korea known under a variety of fanciful names such as Mayflower Viburnum, Fragrant

Viburnum, Pink Snowball, Korean Spice. Its buds are pink, its flowers white and heavenly fragrant. It blooms in May. Most plants from nurseries are grafted. COMPACTA is a low-growing form. Zone 5.

*V. Chenaulti.* More compact version of *V. Burkwoodi.* Zone 5.

*V. fragrans.* Introduced by Reginald Farrer from China. Pale pink to white flowers, very fragrant, before the leaves in late March or early April. Very desirable for the early spring garden but in the North, at least, should be in protected site to prevent the early-developing buds from winterkilling. Zone 6.

*V. Juddi.* Still another hybrid (*V. Carlesi* and *V. Bitchiuense*). Scented flowers and good habit. Zone 5.

*V. odoratissimum.* Sweet Viburnum. Evergreen species from Japan, suitable for South. Handsome foliage, fragrant flower clusters in early spring. Zone 8.

*V. opulus.* European Cranberry. European native grown in various forms in this country since Colonial times. Maplelike foliage and umbels of white flowers, the outer flowers being sterile. Height, about 12 feet. Zone 3. There is a COMPACT form, about 2 feet tall, with red berries. XANTHOCARPUM has yellow berries. Though showy in flower and fruit, the European Cranberry is attacked by aphids that curl the leaves under. The leaves protect the aphids from spray, making it difficult to control them.

*V. tomentosum.* Doublefile Viburnum. Flat clusters of white flowers in late May. the marginal flowers being sterile. Variety MARIESI is choice, its sterile flowers, larger and showier. PINK BEAUTY has flowers that fade to pink. Variety STERILE or PLICATUM, Japanese Snowball, has ball-like clusters of all-sterile white flowers in early June. All of these Viburnums are graceful shrubs with an interesting, horizontal branching habit, eventually reaching about 9 feet. Zone 5.

# VITEX

TYPE Deciduous
FAMILY *Verbenaceae* (Ver-bee-*nay*-see-ee)
GENUS *Vitex* (*Vye*-tex)
SPECIES *agnus-castus* (ag-nus-*kas*-tus), *negundo* (neg-*un*-doh)
ZONE 5, 7

Vitex is a shrub of mid- to late-summer value. Both species are native to southern Europe and Asia. It is sometimes called Chaste-tree.

USES  Place Vitex in the rear or middle of a mixed shrub border to provide midsummer color. It contrasts well with Rose of Sharon. Also use as a background for a flower garden, as an occasional lawn accent, or trained against a wall or fence. Flower spikes are effective in arrangements with Phlox and Day-lilies and with annuals like Marigolds and Zinnias.

HABIT OF GROWTH  Full and spreading in growth, Vitex may reach a height of 10 feet when its stems are not winter-killed, but in northern areas when its stems do die back it remains around 5 or 6 feet high; its spread is about the same.

FLOWERS  The lilac flowers, about ⅓ inch long, appear in tiers on spikes about 7 inches long at the ends of the branches. The flower spikes are larger versions of those of the true Lavender (*Lavendula*). They first appear in midsummer and continue into fall, the greatest display being in late summer.

FOLIAGE  Handsome but tropical-appearing foliage. The opposite, divided leaves, dark green above, gray underneath, are aromatic when crushed and somewhat resemble those of the Japanese Maple (*Acer palmatum*). The number of leaflets varies from three to seven; the average length is about 4 inches.

ASSETS  The contrasting effect of the flower spikes, which help extend the blooming period of the shrub garden, is the main virtue of Vitex. These shrubs are tolerant of sandy soils and seem to do especially well in sheltered seaside gardens.

FAULTS  Their somewhat exotic appearance—mainly due to leaf formation—dictates their careful use around the average home.

CULTURE  Easy to grow in sunny situations in average or even sandy soil. If the soil is very sandy, mix peat moss in the planting hole. Spring planting is recommended over fall plant-ing.

PRUNING  In cold climates, Vitex is best handled as a die-back shrub. In spring, cut the tops off to within a few inches of the ground. New, compact growth will then appear and reach no more than about 6 feet, spreading about as much. In protected areas and in mild climates, Vitex can be shortened or shaped as necessary, the cuts being made back to buds. Growth will be taller and more open.

SPECIES  *Vitex agnus-castus*. Chaste-tree. Hemp-tree. Five to seven leaflets. Flowers from July on. Zone 7.
*V. negundo*. Usually available as variety INCISA. Three to five leaflets, more delicate than preceding. Flower spikes appear a little later and are shorter. Considered slightly hardier. Zone 5.

# *WEIGELA*

TYPE Deciduous
FAMILY *Caprifoliaceae* (Kap-rif-foh-lee-*ay*-see-ee)
GENUS *Weigela* (Wye-*jeel*-uh)
SPECIES *florida* (*flor*-id-uh), *hortensis* (hor-*ten*-siss), *praecox* (*pree*-cox)
ZONE 4

This old-fashioned favorite has had to labor under the name Weigela (it was formerly known as Diervilla), often misspelled and pronounced "Weigelia." One variety, VANICEKI, has been called "Cardinal Shrub." The species are native to parts of Asia but most plants today are of hybrid origin.

USES  Best as a single specimen in any uncrowded situation. Also as accent in an extensive shrub border, but each plant should be allowed to form its distinctive arching habit unimpeded by neighboring shrubs. Variegated foliage varieties make striking accents in green-and-white gardens. Cut flowering branches are most effective in flower arrangements.

HABIT OF GROWTH  Dense, fountainlike form, the branches arching or often sweeping the ground. Height about 3–4 feet to 5–7 feet at maturity.

FLOWERS  Trumpet-shaped, or elongated, bell-shaped flowers, about 1½ inches long, in clusters along the branches, in late spring, early summer and usually intermittently thereafter. Colors are pink, rose, red, and white.

FOLIAGE  Opposite, bright green leaves that clothe the stems and appear before the flowers. There is a variegated leaf form with leaves edged in creamy yellow.

ASSETS  Bountiful flower display that is showy and long lasting plus a graceful habit and winter hardiness.

FAULTS  Weigela needs ample space to assume its handsome form and shouldn't be crowded. In cold regions some branches may winterkill.

CULTURE  Easy in full sun or very light shade in well-drained, moderately rich, moist soil. Add peat moss or compost to planting hole.

PRUNING  If parts of branches or stems have winterkilled in cold regions, cut off such sections as soon as extent of injury has been determined. As plants mature and become crowded, after flowering, remove a few stems at base to force new, strong growth. Also after flowering, shorten portions of stems that have flowered by cutting back to side shoots.

SPECIES AND VARIETIES  *Weigela florida.* Often listed as *W. rosea.* Pink-flowered species from China and Korea, reaching about 8 feet. Variety VARIEGATA has green leaves edged with creamy white. Other varieties, probably hybrids, include BRISTOL RUBY, with ruby-red flowers in late May, hardy and outstanding; EVA RATHKE, standard variety with dark red flowers in June, 3–5 feet high; VANICEKI, bright red flowers in late May, hardier than Bristol Ruby, and called "Cardinal Shrub" by many nurseries; BRISTOL SNOWFLAKE, 1961 introduction from Bristol Nurseries, Bristol, Conn., with pure white flowers in late May on graceful plant.

*W. hortensis.* Species from Japan. NIVEA has white flowers.

*W. praecox.* Species from Korea important as parent of hybrids with preceding species or others not listed here. Varieties or hybrids include AVALANCHE, white, 5–6 feet high. There are many other named Weigela hybrids, but these are the cream of the crop offered by most nurseries today.

# WINTER-HAZEL

TYPE Deciduous
FAMILY *Hamamelidaceae* (Ham-am-mel-id-*day*-see-ee)
GENUS *Corylopsis* (Kor-il-*lop*-siss)
SPECIES *glabrescens* (glab-*ress*-enz), *pauciflora* (paw-sif-*floh*-ruh),
*sinensis* (sin-*nen*-siss), *spicata* (spye-*kay*-tuh), *Willmottiae* (Will-
*mot*-tee-ee)
ZONE 6 and 7

Still another shrub for the collector and winter-weary gardener who enjoys early-flowering plants. The Winter-hazels are native to Asia.

USES   In mixed shrub borders, in groupings with other early-blooming shrubs, or naturalized at the edge of a woodland. They are effective against walls or fences.

HABIT OF GROWTH   Very twiggy, shrubby growth, rounded and dense, some to 6 feet or so, others taller. Most have grayish bark against which the flowers show well.

FLOWERS   Lovely, soft yellow in drooping racemes before the leaves in early spring. They are sweetly scented and can permeate the surrounding area with their perfume.

FOLIAGE   Rather attractive, heart-shaped leaves with strong veins. Leaves may turn to yellow in the fall.

ASSETS   Their early, scented flowers as well as the attractive form of the shrub.

FAULTS   Flowers and buds can be damaged by cold. Gardeners with small properties in cold regions had better forego the Winter-hazel.

CULTURE   Plant in well-drained humusy soil, in full sun or in light, high shade. Try to place them where they receive some protection from winter blasts. Prune after flowering to shape and to keep plants bushy and to remove winter-injured branches, if necessary.

SPECIES   *Corylopsis glabrescens.* Fragrant Winter-hazel. The hardiest and sweetest-scented, to 15 feet. It will thrive in New England or comparable regions where temperatures may drop to 10 degrees below zero. Flowers appear in mid-April, sometimes earlier.

*C. pauciflora.* Buttercup Winter-hazel. Compact and floriferous, to 4 to 6 feet. Not quite as hardy as the preceding; plant in protected spot.

*C. sinensis.* Chinese Winter-hazel. About the same hardiness as the preceding species. Grows to 10 feet.

*C. spicata.* Spike Winter-hazel. Height about 6 feet. A lovely plant, but buds are frequently nipped by cold when temperatures drop to zero.

*C. Willmottiae.* Same attractive flowers and habit (but height to 12 feet) and hardiness as *C. spicata.*

# WINTER JASMINE

TYPE Deciduous
FAMILY *Oleaceae* (Oh-lee-*ay*-see-ee)
GENUS *Jasminum* (*Jass*-min-um)
SPECIES *nudiflorum* (new-dif-*floh*-rum)
ZONE 6

Truly a joy when it bursts into flower—in the North, in early April. Many Jasmines are vines (such as the beloved Poets Jessamine of the South), but this species is more sprawling than vining and with proper pruning appears a mound of gold when in flower. It is native to China.

USES  Ideal against a sunny wall, where it can be espaliered or not, or at the top of a wall or bank where its long shoots can droop gracefully. However, it can be grown as a specimen mounded shrub, with graceful, spreading branches. Cut stems are easily forced into early flowering indoors.

HABIT OF GROWTH  Naturally sprawling, its bright green stems may reach 15 feet if unrestricted, as they root in the ground to form untidy thickets. Such thickets can often be spotted in the southern countryside where Winter Jasmine has escaped from former gardens.

FLOWERS  Bright yellow, tubular flowers, slightly scented, before the leaves, in very early spring.

FOLIAGE  Bright green leaves in threes, after the flowers.

ASSETS  The very early, showy flowers and bright green stems which are attractive in winter.

CULTURE  Winter Jasmine needs full sun and in the North does best when given some protection, the flowers then appearing that much earlier. It will survive occasional winter temperatures to 10 degrees below zero.

PRUNING  Cut out old stems occasionally after flowering, cutting back to ground level. Shorten stems as necessary for training.

# *WINTERSWEET*

TYPE Deciduous
FAMILY *Calycanthaceae* (Kal-ik-kanth-*ay*-see-ee)
GENUS *Chimonanthus* (Kye-mon-*anth*-us)
SPECIES *praecox* (*pree*-cox)
ZONE 7

Haunting and unforgettable can be the sweet scent of Winter-sweet, a native of China.

USES This is a shrub for the collector as well as the indomitable gardener who loves a garden stroll in even the meanest early spring weather, for this shrub often flowers in January or February in the vicinity of Long Island and coastal New Jersey. Branches can be cut all through the winter and placed in water, and they will then fill a room with fragrance. It is not especially prized other than for its fragrance, so the garden use of Wintersweet is limited to locating it where it will have good protection and be inconspicuous the remainder of the year.

HABIT OF GROWTH Rounded, shrubby habit; reaches 4 to 5 feet, although it may go to 8 feet in mild climates.

FLOWERS Pale-yellow flowers, with purple or brown centers, about 1 inch across and a little like those of the Strawberry-shrub, of which it is a near relative. They are not especially beautiful, but show up readily enough on the winter-bare branches. However, who cares about their appearance? The delicious and pervasive Honeysuckle scent makes up for the lack of special beauty.

FOLIAGE Rough-textured, bright green leaves in opposite arrangement.

ASSETS Wintersweet adds scent and, therefore, interest to the garden in winter and early spring.

FAULTS Not for regions where temperatures remain long below zero, as obviously buds and flowers can be easily injured.

CULTURE Wintersweet likes a southern and protected exposure and a light, well-drained soil. It will take part shade in summer. One way of growing Wintersweet is against a wall, in which case shoots that have flowered can be cut back nearly to the main stem. The new growth will bear the next crop of flowers.

# *WITCH-HAZEL*

TYPE Deciduous
FAMILY *Hamamelidaceae* (Ham-am-mel-id-*day*-see-ee)
GENUS *Hamamelis* (Ham-am-*meel*-iss)
SPECIES *japonica* (jap-*pon-ik*-uh), *mollis* (*moll*-iss), *vernalis* (ver-*nay*-liss), *virginiana* (vir-jin-ee-*ay*-nuh)
ZONE 4

Unique are the Witch-hazels—one species has the distinction of being about the earliest to bloom of early spring-flowering shrubs, while another species is about the last shrub to flower in the fall. This widely distributed plant, which has species native to North America as well as to China and Japan, is a great favorite and for good reason.

USES These shrubs need lots of room—plant in open woodlands, along boundaries, and in backgrounds of shrub borders. Useful for simple indoor arrangements at a time when the garden offers little, if any, cutting material.

HABIT OF GROWTH They vary greatly in habit according to origin and training, but are generally open and spreading, sometimes even straggly. Heights vary from 6 to 10 to 25 feet or so.

FLOWERS Curious flowers with narrow, twisted petals like ribbons. Their general effect is spidery. They can be delightfully fragrant, with their scent being especially appreciated when branches are brought indoors. The usual color is yellow, although there are a few varieties with reddish tones. In the case of *Hamamelis virginiana,* ripening capsular fruits from the previous year's flowering are often seen together with the current flowers.

FOLIAGE The leaves, which appear after the flowers in the spring-blooming kinds, are alternate and turn to yellow, orange, or purple in the fall.

ASSETS Their unusual blooming seasons, which make it possible to have shrubs in flower in cold months in the North; also the fragrance of their flowers. They are very hardy and free from pests and diseases.

FAULTS Witch-hazels are not for very small properties, nor are they for those who feel little or no concern for all-season gardens. While their flowers are charming and showy for the periods in which they appear, they do not have the flamboyance of a Lilac, a Rhododendron, or a Forsythia.

CULTURE   The Witch-hazels are easy to grow and can be safely planted out in the spring or fall. They have no special soil requirements, merely needing the usual good drainage. Very heavy clay soils or those that are especially sandy should have peat moss or compost added to the planting hole. Witch-hazels will grow in sun or light shade.

PRUNING   Occasional removal of straggly branches or, if Witch-hazels are being trained to grow like small trees with a single trunk, removal of side branches in the spring.

SPECIES AND VARIETIES   *Hamamelis japonica.* Japanese Witch-hazel. Lemon-yellow flowers, fragrant, from December to March, depending on climate and weather. Its ultimate height may be 20 feet. ARBOREA, described as more vigorous in growth, and FLAVO PURPURESCENS, with red-tinted petals, are varieties. *H. mollis.* Chinese Witch-hazel. Perhaps the best species, and available from most nurseries. Golden-yellow flowers, with dark-red calyx, very fragrant. Larger leaves than the others, gray underneath. Ultimate height 10 to 12 feet, higher in the South. Variety BREVIPETALA has shorter, orange-tinged petals. *H. vernalis.* Vernal Witch-hazel. Native to Missouri and bordering states. Its flowers are smaller than those of the Chinese Witch-hazel but are very fragrant and may appear as early as January in the North. Its height is about 6 feet, and as it produces many shoots from the base, it is best used in woodlands or naturalistic plantings. *H. virginiana.* Virginian Witch-hazel. Native to eastern North American woodlands. Flowers, less showy than others, appear in late fall, usually before the foliage has fallen. Leaves turn bright yellow. Its bark and leaves are ingredients of the astringent remedy witch-hazel, familiar in most households.

*SOURCES OF FLOWERING SHRUBS*

ALEXANDER, J. HERBERT
Middleboro, Massachusetts
(Lilacs)

ARMSTRONG NURSERIES
Ontario, California
(General)

BALDSIEFEN, WARREN
89 Forest Place, Rochelle Park, New Jersey
(Azaleas and Rhododendrons)

BOVEES, THE
S.W. Coronado & 16th Drive, Portland, Oregon
(Azaleas, Rhododendrons, and related plants)

BRAND PEONY FARMS
Box 408, Fairbault, Minnesota
(Lilacs)

BRIMFIELD GARDENS NURSERY
245 Brimfield Road, Wethersfield, Connecticut
(General, Unusual)

CLARENDON GARDEN NURSERY
Box 1071, Pinehurst, North Carolina
(Camellias, Azaleas)

COLEMAN, S. D., NURSERIES
Fort Gaines, Georgia
(Camellias, Azaleas)

COMERFORD'S
P. O. Box 100, Marion, Oregon
(Azaleas, Rhododendrons)

ENGLISH, CARL
8546 30th Avenue N.W., Seattle 7, Washington
(Azalea, Rhododendron Seeds)

GABLE, JOSEPH B.
Stewartstown, Pennsylvania
(Azaleas and Rhododendrons)

GIRARD BROS. NURSERY
Geneva, Ohio
(General)

HEARD'S LANDSCAPE NURSERIES
4727 Beaver Avenue, Des Moines 11, Iowa
(Lilacs)

HOLLY HILL FARM NURSERY
Straight Path Road, R.D. 4, Huntington, Long Island, New York
(Heaths, Heathers, and Related Plants)

INTERSTATE NURSERIES
Hamburg, Iowa
(General)

KANSAS LANDSCAPE & NURSERY CO.
1416 East Iron, Salina, Kansas
(General)

KELLY BROS. NURSERY
Dansville, New York
(General)

KELSEY NURSERY SERVICE
104 Portland Road, Highlands, New Jersey
(General)

KERN, JOSEPH J.
Box 33, Mentor, Ohio
(Shrub Roses)

KINGSVILLE NURSERY
Kingsville, Maryland
(General)

LA BAR'S RHODODENDRON NURSERY
Stroudsburg, Pennsylvania
(Native Azaleas and Rhododendrons)

LAMB NURSERIES
Spokane 2, Washington
(General)

LESLIE WILD FLOWER NURSERY
30 Sumner, Methuen, Massachusetts
(Trailing-Arbutus, Bunchberry, etc.)

MAYFAIR NURSERY
R.D. 2, Nichols, New York
(Heaths and Heathers, Dwarf Shrubs)

OLIVER AND SIMSON NURSERIES
313 Central Avenue, Scarsdale, New York
(Azaleas, Rhododendrons, Rare Plants)

SAXTON AND WILSON
Maplewood, Oregon
(General, Unusual)

SHERIDAN NURSERIES, LTD.
Box 181, Toronto 18, Ontario, Canada
(General)

LOUIS SMIRNOW
Linden Lane, Glen Head, Long Island, New York
(Tree Peonies)

STARK BROS. NURSERIES
Box 795, Louisiana, Missouri
(General)

STONECROP NURSERIES
R. F. D. 1, Cold Spring, New York
(Dwarf Shrubs, Genista, etc.)

THOMASVILLE NURSERIES
Thomasville, Georgia
(General)

TILLOTSON, WILL, ROSE GARDENS
802 Brown Valley Road, Watsonville, California
(Shrub Roses)

TINGLE'S NURSERY
Pittsville, Maryland
(General)

WAYSIDE GARDENS
Mentor, Ohio
(General, Unusual)

WESTON NURSERIES
Hopkinton, Massachusetts
(General)

WHITE FLOWER FARM
Litchfield, Connecticut
(General, Unusual)

# INDEX